SURVIVING THE MOURNING

By Lori Grasman

Lori.
I was drawn to this book for you
I hope it helps in some way.
I'm here for you.
Love
Tina

DEDICATION

I dedicate this book to my Son Darien Grasman
You will always be..My Life, My Heart until my Last Breath
Wait for me to come home

Love Mom xxxxooo

Till Our Eyes Meet, You Won't Ever Be Alone and If You Hurt Me, That's Ok Baby Only
Words Bleed, Inside These Pages You Just Hold Me, and I Won't Ever Let You Go
WAIT FOR ME TO COME HOME

This is My Precious Son, Darien

CONTENTS

A Parent
Never Expects
To Lose
A Child
So Please
Be Kind
To Them

I needed Kindness
Not Opinions

ACKNOWLEDGMENTS

Acknowledgments

I must first thank Terry Daly, my friend and the extremely talented artist who let me have and use the drawing which was used for the front cover. Terry, thank you we both know that this was the heart of the matter. Your drawing resonated deep inside to the root of my pain over losing my Son Darien. You made the original drawing after losing your Mom and with a heart of gold you shared your pain with me and through me. And in between everything, you lost your beautiful Sister 1 year after I lost my Son on the same exact date. The drawing holds so much meaning between us.. Love you Girlie..xo

I must also thank my Best friend Laura who I have known since I was about 7 years old. Her parents were my second set of parents and I loved them dearly, God Bless them both. Thank you for being there consistently throughout the loss of my Darien. You and Jimmy have given me a place to stay for the funeral arrangements(which was the hardest thing I ever had to go through in my life) You left me alone when I needed to isolate and you were there when I needed to vent and fall apart. I was so emotionally destroyed inside and I know it was hard on you watching me try to keep myself from breaking down. There was no way that I could have purchased a dress for Darien's funeral, (I couldn't deal with it) Thank you for lending me one of yours of which I wore both days. You allowed our whole family to come and go from your house as needed and you always offered us food and lots of love.

 My family was so heartbroken over my Son's death, thank you for letting me invite myself back whenever I needed to see my daughters Danelle and Dakota Rose. It was very hard going back and forth from another State. You allowed me to treat your home like it was my home and I truly needed that because I felt so displaced during that time. I had just moved to Florida and two months later my Son died, it has changed my life forever. I went from extremely happy to extremely devastated in one day. I will never be exactly who I was, that perSon died with my Son. Thank you for being so kind and loving to my children, I know you always had a special place in your heart for Darien, as we all did. We know each other for over 49 years and I think you only saw me cry 3 times, so I know when I lost it you were scared for me, I was scared for myself, after all I've always been the "I'm ok" friend. After losing Darien I held myself together as long as I could . He will always be the missing piece to my heart. We both know that I was always worried about him and that I always feared this would happen. Thank you for being there throughout the nightmare of the hardest thing I ever went through.. Love you Always xo

I thank my friend Michele who is always up all hours of the night, always there to talk with me and acknowledge my feelings with respect. Michele knew how to give an opinion and express an idea without taking away what I was feeling. She made my (feeling crazy days) into (it's just a bad day and it will pass) day. Michele, you have always had my back no matter what and you were always there to help me look at the other side of things when I found it hard to. Michele you always had kind things to say and always supported my ideas and truly enjoyed my perSonality.

Thank you to my friend Rose for all of the times I needed to vent, you listened so patiently and had so much wisdom and unselfish advice. You have such a gentle way with words and your very sincere.

Thank you to my friend Janet who is so sweet and unselfish and called me so many times to check on me. You showed so much concern, sometimes I had to console you, even though you called to console me. You are so deeply emotional and that makes you so beautiful. You could never tell a lie, and I love that about you.

I must now thank Sharon, my neighbor for being there for me the minute I found out about my Son. She helped me book my flight to get home as soon as I could. She remained so calm that it helped me to focus the best I could. I'll always admire her for that. Sadly she recently passed away.. Love you Sharon, miss you..God Bless

Thank you to my fiend Linda who came over right away and waited with me to take me to the airport to go back to New York at 4am.

And to all of the people who came to my Son's funeral thank you so much, as devastating as it was, all of you made it so beautiful. I was so amazed by the amount of people who showed up to Honor his life and Death. I loved hearing each and every one of you talk about my Son Darien. All of your beautiful words and stories helped make my Son Darien's life matter and have so much meaning. I know he was watching over us as an Angel and feeling so proud to see all of you there to say goodbye and honor his life. Even through my deepest pain I aimed at making his funeral as unique s my Son Darien was, (and it was). I know for sure it's how he would have wanted it to be. Love you all..xo

CHAPTER 1 WITH LOVE, TO DARIEN LOVE MOM

From the moment I knew I was pregnant with you I knew you were going to be a boy. I talked to my belly many times and sang Songs to you. I found so much joy in watching you develop. From the stages of crawling, walking and talking you had your own unique style. From an early age you always knew how to capture everyone's attention with your beautiful smile and your adorable laugh. You were always very strong minded and you held a powerful presence from a very young age. Early on you learned to use your squeaky voice to get what you wanted from me, although as you got older I somehow caught on. You were so bright and you were always trying to learn something new. I was so amazed how you became so open with your feelings and how you always shared them with me. (When you hurt) (I hurt).

I am forever grateful that you were my Son, as you certainly made life interesting. You never judged anyone and that helped you to develop many strong relationships with people from all different backgrounds, which I found to be awesome. I remember fighting with you tooth and nail to keep your job in the beginning. Eventually you realized the value of that job and stuck it out and everything worked out well. I'm so proud of you for hanging in there and trusting that eventually you would really like your job and all that it had to offer. You made so many great friends on that job and you earned so much respect from your co workers and bosses. All of them had such good things to say about you and that you were such a good worker. You have made your mark in this world Darien, I'm so proud of you.

This book was made In Honor of Your Life and the beautiful way in which you have made your mark in this world. You have touched the hearts of so many people. I don't think you ever realized the depth of who you were to others and how you affected the people around you and those in your life. But I know you know now and I hope you are smiling as you watch all of us connect with each other over you as we share the essence of your life.

Without my spirituality I would be with you right now, it's what keeps me here with your sisters, as they need me more than ever now. You have brought so much meaning to my life and I thank you for sharing your life with me. It's now almost a year since you passed and yet it feels like it just happened. Every day I wake up and as I look around and see traces of your life I am reminded all over again that you are no longer physically here. That part hurts the most because there is nothing I can do to change it.

I miss your voice, your smile, your laughter and the funny faces you would make when you felt like being silly. I miss your face and your beautiful big brown eyes and I hate that I can no longer see them in front of me. I miss (MY SON) (My Heart).

Honoring Darien

This book was written to Honor my Son "Darien Grasman" who left my life on July 24th-25th 2015, I use both dates because the accident was on July 24th at night and he was in a coma and was taken off life support before 12am but the hospital took time with the paperwork because we decided to donate what could be used to help others in need, so officially the death certificate was documented 12:14 am the next day on the 25th of July. But for me, spiritually he left his body when his heart stopped. Though for legal purposes we are forced to use the official date. I did try to fight them over this but the hospital said that it would be a lot of work to correct 14 minutes on a death certificate and change the date. My Darien will never be forgotten and a huge piece of my heart will always be missing. He was my first beautiful experience of being a Mother and being the first grandchild and nephew on his Dad's side. It hurts to think of all of the future events that will come up and happen without him being there, although I know in spirit he will always be there watching us.

I am so thankful for all of the signs he sends me along the way because they help me hold myself together. He was and will always be such a precious Soul and I am so extremely thankful to have been his Mom. His personality will live on through each and every beautiful vivid memory I have of him. And for the rest of my life I will replay them to keep him alive in my mind. It gives me a place to go when I feel distraught and cannot handle the reality of his death. It's something I must live through while my thoughts fight my heart over what should have been or could have been. It's a struggle every day, acceptance is always a struggle. God had other plans for my Son and I must accept that. I am grateful to have had him for the 26 years in my life. I would rather have had him and lost him then to never have had him at all. All Blessings have expirations dates, we just don't know who and when. God Bless all parents out there, may this never be your cross to bear.

There have been parents before me who have lost a child and there will be parents after me and I pray they have a good support system and good friends. I thank God so many good caring people came forward to let me know they were there for me when and if I needed them. I was fortunate to have created many strong and valued friendships along the way and I truly appreciate each and every one of them for being there for me. In reincarnation it says that we will all experience everything that happens in life so that we can grow and learn from the experience. If this is true, then I hope that in my future live I will never have to lose a child again. As I said I thank God for my spirituality because it has been the main thing that has kept me humble to the fact that God's decision will always supersede all decisions and outcomes, after all my Son Darien belonged to God first and then God picked me to be Darien's Mom to take care of him and love him while he is on Earth.

I started to write this book soon after my Son passed away, but in between the stress and anxiety of losing him I could not even breathe long enough to think. My emotions were in a deep state of turmoil. So it has taken me well over a year to gather all of my heartfelt thoughts and emotional pain and put it all together, first as a journal and then sorting it all out in a timeline manor and thus eventually creating this book. The main purpose of this book is to share my experience and pain with other parents out there who before me and after me have lost a child and who are now on this heart wrenching road ahead, and to honor my Son Darien, my beautiful first born child who I waited for my whole life. Who will always be so deeply embedded in my memory forever.

Ever since I was a little girl I always dreamed of being married one day and having children. I myself was the oldest child in my family and I always remember wishing I had an older brother to protect me and look after me, so in the dreamy planning of my future I always prayed that my first child would be a boy because I wanted my future daughters to have a big brother. Being so young my thoughts for the future only went so far (in my head). Although I also dreamed I would marry a Prince Charming and live happily ever after. As I got older reality kicked in and life was not as simple as my dreams. Marriage and having children required more than just waking up to a dreamy perfect world, it took effort and sacrifice and learning to look beyond myself. When I eventually had children my whole heart immediately absorbed every part of their being into the greatest love that I would ever have had experienced in my entire life. They became my reason to have a better life and everything I did was for them and their future.

I wanted them to have everything they needed and I promised myself to give them all of the beautiful experiences that I had missed out on, like the love, the hugs, the hope, the joyful tears of pride and self love and the feeling that someone will always have their back. I always wanted them to feel safe and of course I wanted them to have long and happy lives. So that meant my job was to keep them alive no matter what. So when I lost my Son Darien, there was this little inside voice that said (I was supposed to keep him alive) and in that moment I wished I had the power to fight God and yell out (I want my Son back, you made a mistake) but I know deep down inside that God does what is best for us in order for us to continue our journey of learning and optimal growth. There is always a great purpose in everything that he does, so I silently hang on to four faithful words "Thy Will Be Done", and in that moment I try to surrender and leave it all in God's hands.

So I will begin by telling you that my Son Darien was my first child, he was born on September 14th 1988 in Lenox hill Hospital in Manhattan New York. When I gave birth to him he was 6lbs 21 inches long and he had these beautiful brown eyes that were so huge. His eyes were so captivating that when he looked at me I almost felt as if he were about to say something profound, his expressions were so adult like. He was such an enjoyable baby and he loved when I would talk or sing to him. His favorite Song was "Sherry" by Frankie Valli, he always got so excited listening to it and he would shake his whole body when I played or sang that Song to him. I had selected his name when I was 21 years old, I lived on the 3rd floor of an apartment building and my neighbor Doreen who lived one floor below me just gave birth to a baby boy. She named him Darien and he was such a good baby, always smiling. I enjoyed visiting him and watching him grow. It was in those moments that I decided that one day my first child was going to be a boy and I was going to name him Darien.

About 7 years later I was married and I later gave birth to "my Darien" and low and behold he too smiled all the time and was such a happy baby. He was always so thrilled with whatever we gave him to play with. Darien became the deepest part of my heart and no one in my entire life had ever entered the area of my heart that became his. He was such a bright child and very ahead of his time. He was always trying to figure something out and learn. He was so smart that he had to be kept busy most of the time or he would become easily bored and distracted and move on to something else. He had been diagnosed with ADD (Attention Deficit Disorder) at an early age so we had to keep him involved with stimulating projects which helped challenge him and gave him many choices to keep him interested and help him to use his creativity productively or he would become very frustrated. It certainly explained his desire for so many hobbies and his need for wanting to do everything perfectly. He loved skateboarding, racing cars, drifting, BMX biking, and motorcycles, which last but not least is what led to the nightmare and drastic change our live were about to go through. From that moment our lives changed drastically and very fast. In the blink of an eye I was forced to accept the unacceptable, the loss of my beautiful Son and the loss of the old me. Right before that I had just sold my house in Seaford New York and bought a condo in Delray Beach Florida. In that moment my children were doing fine. Everyone was happy and healthy. My daughter Danelle was living in Melville New York with her fiancé Adam(who I've grown to love so much) and my Son Darien had his own apartment in Bay Shore New York and my daughter Dakota Rose was originally going to move with me to Florida but then chose to stay in Commack New York at my friend Laura's house. So to me everything was fine, my children were grown and moving along in their lives. My daughters had come to visit right after I moved and my Son said he was planning to visit me soon. My daughter Danelle was having her engagement party on July 11th 2015 so I had my flight already booked to go back for the party. The engagement party eventually came and things were going well. I remember sitting at the table staring at my Son from a distance and thinking how handsome he looked and how he was maturing so quickly.

Their Dad was able to come to the party, he had been away and had not seen them for almost 2 years and I believe we all shared a mixed and anxious feeling of seeing him for the first time and more so because it would be in front of so many people. There were so many questions that could not be asked because it was a party. But the moment he walked in we all greeted him as if no time had passed. I remember tearing up when my daughters hugged him hello and I was happy that everything worked out and that there were no awkward moments. After all it was a party. The party was moving along and everyone was having a good time. They were now serving coffee and cake and some people were starting to leave. I remember giving my Son a great big hug not knowing that it would be the last hug we would ever share between us. I returned to Florida a few days after the party. My children were going about their usual routines and everyone was fine. I remember my Son calling me one night and he was upset about his relationship, I told him to calm down and that everyone had ups and downs, he told me he wanted to get away to clear his head so I told him that he could always come by me for a break. He agreed and said he would think about it and that he would Call me back.

The next and last phone was him telling me that he was going to try and work things out in his life. I told him that only he knows what he can handle and what will work best for him, he thanked me for listening to him and being there for him. That was the last time I heard his voice. As a Mother my instinct is to take away any pain that my children go through and could ever have, but I stayed un involved and I respected his decision . I remember being younger and having those on and off again relationships, the back and forth dance of break up to make up. Sometimes they just need a little space. So by now it was July 24th and I just finished meeting up with two of my friends and having a great lunch in Boca Raton Florida, we were laughing so hard and telling stories and having so much fun. Lunch was done and we all had to get back home so I got in my car to drive home. I remembered thinking that my life seemed so perfect I was in a beautiful area, the weather was great most of the time. That day it started to pour very hard but it had stopped by the time I got home. It was still early and the rain had stopped so I decided to walk around my development for a while and stop by the pool area to see if anyone was there that I knew. It was kind of empty, as I'm sure it was because of all of the rain.

I found it funny how the pool was usually always filled with people but no one ever swims, they just stand in one spot and talk to each other. If you want to swim you have to swim around them. At this point I decided to go back home and check to see if I had any mail. I then returned to my condo and put the TV on.

I was really enjoying my day and loving my new condo, I think that what I liked the most is that it had 2 bathrooms. In New York you're lucky if a 3 bedroom house has 2 bathrooms. I finally had my very own bathroom that no one else would ever use. Honestly I was at the height of my happiness and in that moment everything seemed so perfect. No complaints in my corner, I think I was glowing with relief from not having all the stress and bills from when I lived in New York. My car and condo were paid for and I realized I could actually breathe again. Financially a huge weight was lifted off my shoulders.

CHAPTER 2 THE DEVASTATING PHONE CALL

I was home about 4 hours when my phone rang, on the other end was my daughter Danelle. She called me to tell me that my Son Darien was in an accident and that she would get more information and call me back. In my mind I remembered that he had been in other accidents in the past and that he was always alright. Except for the last accident, he actually broke the bone in his calf and it took months to heal. I thought for sure after that accident that he would not ride anymore, but no, not my Son, he goes out and buys a brand new(Red Ducati) after his leg healed. My daughter called me back and proceeded to tell me that he was airlifted to Stony Brook Hospital. Now my mind was racing, I still tried to convince myself that they airlift as a protocol for motorcycle accidents to be safe and quickly get them to a hospital and that he was going to be alright. I was also thinking how far away I was and if I should I be booking a flight home and I was also wondering how serious it was. Danelle told me she will find out more and call me back right away. I kept thinking " this cannot be happening", and then my thoughts went to (he is going to be fine).

I was now nervously waiting for my daughters phone call and for her to tell me that he was going to be ok.. When my daughter called me back she was more upset now and she told me that he just arrived at Stony Brook Hospital and the doctors said he is in a coma and will need to be placed on life support. Hearing those words on the other side of the phone while I was miles away was so crushing and immensely painful. In that moment in time everything in my life was frozen, time had completely stopped, my heart stopped and shock took over, I honestly could not breathe, at least I don't remember breathing. I could hear what my daughter was telling me but my mind was not allowing it to register in my head. I thought again about all of the other accidents he had been in and I thought (he will be ok), just like all of the other times.

It was then that my daughter put the doctor on the phone to speak to me, I was hoping that he was going to say that there was a mistake and that Darien was fine, but no, not this time. He said that Darien was in a coma and had suffered severe brain damage and that his organs were beginning to shut down. This was all too much to take in, my baby was miles away and about to die. So at this point I was sick to my stomach. I felt as if my whole life itself was being terminated, voided out and I would soon no longer have my precious Son. My life's dream and plan was now forever changed, my whole purpose in life was being erased in the blink of an eye. I felt so sick, I kept thinking to myself " I was supposed to keep him alive", that's what parents do and they don't ever outlive their children. We are supposed to help them grow and mature and set them up to move forward without us, not the other way around. It should have been my death, not his. He should have been the one planning my funeral, not me "his Mother" planning his! I was supposed to get old and see him get married and have children.

He was supposed to come to me for advice when times got rough. My thoughts were racing all over the place and I now had to get on a plane as quickly as possible. I needed to be with him and hold him in his last moments. God I needed to be there that second. I remembered a conversation I had with my Son a few years back where he talked about what a great Dad he was going to be one day when he had children. He made it sound like being a parent was going to be so easy. I remembered laughing and telling him to wait and see how much work was involved. I was so set in my mind on seeing it all come to life one day and now to receive this final blow of reality telling me that it will never happen. It was so very painful emotionally..

The reality was that he was never going to have children or get to enjoy raising them and that I would never get to be a Grandmother to his children "hurt like hell" , I kept telling myself "just keep breathing" because I felt as if I was going to have a heart attack. I was so confused at this point an didn't know what to do, one moment I was so extremely happy and my life was going great and the next moment I was losing my Son, it was a horrible nightmare. Southwest tried their best to get me on the last flight that night but I was too far away and they could not hold a plane for that long so I had the first flight in the morning. I was so destroyed thinking he might die before I get there. The next couple of hours were going to be long and intensely painful. It was such a trapped feeling, there was nothing I could do and no way to get there sooner. I had been communicating back and forth with my daughter Danelle and the doctor wanted to speak with me again. He told me that the life support was just keeping Darien's body alive and that his organs were shutting down quickly.

So at that point I asked the doctor if there was any part of him that could be donated, and he told me that my Son's eyes, skin and heart muscles could still be saved and donated. He then reminded me that Darien was having a heart attack every 5 minutes and that every time they used the drug to stop the heart attacks it hurts what can be donated and that I needed to make a decision as soon as possible about the donation. I was besides myself trying to make a decision, there was a part of me that wanted him to stay on life support until I got there "no matter what", after all I wanted to see my baby and hold him one last time. I was told that 6 doctors confirmed that there would never be any activity in his brain again. As much as I wanted to keep him there long enough for me to get there, my spirituality told me that it was better to help whoever needed the donation. So it was the hardest decision in my life to make the decision to end his life support. I won't lie, I wanted so hard to be selfish just to spend even 2 seconds with him, but I also believed he already left his body.

While they were about to stop the life support my daughter put her phone by my Son's ear while they shut it off and I yelled into the phone " I love you so much Darien, everything is going to be alright " as I was crying. In a matter of minutes the heart attacks took over and he stopped breathing. God I wanted to die with him. That brief moment determined life and death, one moment he was alive, the next moment there was no life left, my precious baby, my Son was gone. I felt so broken and I still had a few hours before going to the airport and I was so confused as to what I should pack, how do you pack for a funeral for your own child?. I don't really remember packing but I do recall thinking that I could not put a black dress in my suitcase, I was so in denial even though I was aware that I now had to plan a funeral, just the thought of it sent me into tears. I actually have no memory of how I packed or what I took with me.

I finally arrived at the airport and had to wait for the departure time. I remember getting on the plane and thinking "no one on this plane knows that I just lost my Son, how can I act like this didn't happen and hold it together?" I had this overwhelming urge to be comforted as I sat on this plane full of strangers. I sat next to this couple that of course had no idea I just lost my Son. They just sat there smiling, probably looking forward to some vacation they were on. For some reason I turned to the lady next to me and I asked her if she had any children. She said she had two children and then she asked me if I had any. I had this need to tell her, it was more of a desperate need, so I said "yes, I have three children, two girls and a boy and that my Son died a few hours ago". She started to cry so hard which in turn made me cry more despite the valium I had taken. Her husband looked over with concern as to why we were both crying and she told him what happened and then he too started crying. I believe in that moment I was in a severe need of recognition over what happened.

Those two people were so humble to my situation with the painful loss of my Son and I believe it helped me feel acknowledged for what I was going through and it helped me deal with being stuck on the plane. It also helped me to get off the plane at the end of the flight and pull myself together a little more and do what I do best, (get through) (not over) whatever was next. I had to be the strong one, and when called upon to do so, that's who I am. Thank God my daughter Danelle and her fiancé Adam were there with my Son until the end. I know that he knew they were both there right beside him. I'm sure that it was hard for them to be there watching him on life and knowing inside that he was not going to make it. My youngest daughter Dakota Rose was stuck in Oswego with a 7 hour drive and no one went out of their way to reach his Father. Before anyone else, his Dad should have been there. Someone should have went to where he was staying and picked him up. I pray that he doesn't carry the guilt of not being able to be there, Darien knows his Dad would have been there if he could. And me as you know, I was stuck waiting for a plane.

CHAPTER 3   GOING TO THE MORGUE

By the next morning we all eventually met up with each other and found out that he was no longer in the hospital and that he was taken to the Morgue. So we now had to go to the Morgue and sign some papers and to see my Son's body. When we arrived at the Morgue they made us wait a little while and then this woman came out to greet us and ask us who we were. I personally found the woman at the Morgue to be rather rude because when we requested to see my Son Darien, she said " you don't want to see him, we just did the autopsy and it's best to wait until the funeral", in my mind I already had this woman's hair ripped out. I turned to her and I said "I don't care what you think, this is our Son and we want to see him no matter what". She still tried to convince us otherwise but I demanded to see my Son. So she reluctantly went back inside to get him ready for us to see him.

She came back out and brought us into a room with a big window with curtains on the other side which were blocking the glass window. Then the curtains opened and his Dad and I were standing there looking at our Son's body on a table. I must tell you that he looked so beautiful . He looked like he was just sleeping, he was so peaceful looking. I thought to myself "what a beautiful face he has". His hair was the way he normally wore it. His skin coloring was so even. He looked like an angel in a deep sleep. I wanted to scream out to him and say "get up now and stop joking around", but inside I knew he was not joking around, he was gone. It all kind of reminded me of the sleeping scene in Snow White, only the poisonous apple was a motorcycle and there was no kiss that would ever wake him up. Reality started to kick in a lot quicker as we were watching him lay there so still. All of his personality drained from his very being, a body with its Soul already gone. I'm sure he was now watching us watching him.

We could have stood there forever because leaving meant a forever of not seeing him. That was the last time I saw my Son Darien. If his Dad and I were able to be at the hospital maybe we would not have had this need to see him at the morgue. But I am still glad I got to see him, he really did look so beautiful like an Angel sleeping, our Angel.

CHAPTER 4 ENTERING HIS APARTMENT

As we arrived at his apartment I remember thinking about how intrusive it felt to open his door without him being there. It almost felt as if we were breaking in and going through his things. To us they were just things, but to him everything in there was a piece of his life and his love of life. I remember walking into his kitchen and looking around and seeing the utensils, tea pot, his pots and pans and the cute little clock on the wall . I felt so distraught knowing that he will never touch these things again. He will never again heat up the tea pot and make me a cup of tea like he used to when I came by. When I went into his bedroom I saw the comforter that I just bought him last Christmas. It was so soft and furry and I knew he would love it and enjoying sleeping in it. I remember breathing it in as I held it because it smelled just like him. I looked around at all of the shoes, shirts and different colored sneakers he had that would never be worn by him again. It was all so heart breaking and sad that his life and future came to a halt.

Going into the bathroom it dawned on me that he was not a little boy, he was a man. I noticed the shaving cream and the masculine hand towels, but I could not help but think of him as my little boy, my baby. As I was going through some of his stuff , even though he was my Son, it still felt so personal and intrusive. It dawned on me that one day we will all die and someone will be going through our belongings. He had a whole life going on in that apartment, brand new TV and living room set. His style was now being taken apart, by us his family and his personality was now being removed from his apartment. Once again it was extremely heart breaking. We still had to go through his drawers and empty what was left in his refrigerator. His wallet was lying on the table in his living room with his license and credit cards along with his last receipt for

Dunkin Donuts, waiting on the table for him to come home. His cologne lingered in the air, a smell that I loved and could never and will never forget. Going through the closet and seeing all of his dressed shirts made me almost lose it emotionally. He looked so handsome in those shirts.

I remember touching his guitar and realizing that I will never hear him play it again or hear him sing a new Song "any Song". He had so much stuff. I remember when he first rented the apartment we went shopping together and I bought him some pictures for the wall, some rugs, pots and pans, and food. I told him I would do that for the first time. He was so excited to decorate the apartment. I also remember coming over after he put his rugs down and I was asked to take my shoes off. Now it was his turn to tell me to take my shoes off. I was so happy my little boy was growing up.. I was so proud of him, he had a great job and things were going well. He had all his toys and he even added a Mercedes to his collection. He was developing into an awesome individual, a beautiful human being. I loved talking about him to everyone. Back at the apartment and going through things I was still very numb at this point and we were all still in shock still trying to figure out what we should do next.

My daughters and I decided to sleep at his apartment in his room the first night. All three of us slept in his bed and tried to breathe in his every being. I hoped that when I woke up in the morning I would find him in the living room sleeping on the couch. But when the morning came we woke up still missing a Son and a Brother. I guess our last hope of it all being a bad dream didn't happen. So we got out of bed and packed the comforter and pillows. The last thing left to do was clean the bathroom and to put the other stuff into bags. We decided to give two of his helmets to his closest friends. They were so happy to receive them. His friends were so helpful throughout it all.

The worst part was going to the Police Dept. to pick up the clothes he died in and his helmet. It's like they just handed us this bag with his clothes and his riding shoes. We just stood there with blank looks on our faces. It felt to me like they were saying "that's it, that's all that's left to him". I didn't even want to touch it because of the finality of it. At that moment denial was a safer place for me. The sadness is so deep that it penetrates a resonating pain right through your very core. All of my dreams with my Son were gone just like that. I now had to plan a funeral. What the hell did I know about funerals, especially for my child. The thought never entered my mind.

CHAPTER 5 THE FUNERAL

Here I was in this new position of a Mother who just lost a child. Not for one second did I blame God or was I mad at God. My spirituality saved my life. Everyone in our family was so affected by this tragedy and loss. When I thought about where I was going to have his funeral I remembered going to a funeral that my one of my friends had when he lost his daughter Samantha (Sammy), it was so heart breaking. I knew her for years. I had even done her hair a few times. She was so sweet and likable. Her personality was the female version of my Son's personality, so outgoing and funny, so full of life. She had a great presence and stood out in a crowd. I felt so sad that she had passed, she was too young. The funeral her Dad planned for her was so beautiful and I always remembered that. So that is how and why I chose to have my Son Darien's funeral at Charles R Boyd Spencer Funeral home in Babylon New York. They arranged everything just the way we wanted it. They were kind and considerate and very delicate in explaining everything to me and had answered all of my questions. They didn't even bring up anything about money throughout the planning. This was the first time I was going through something like this and I pray "the last".

Everything felt as if it was happening in slow motion and losing a child can cause such a destruction of faith along with trying to accept what has just happened. Being the main person making all of the decisions it put a lot of pressure on me to make the right decisions, decisions that would hold no regrets. I kept asking myself "how would Darien have wanted his funeral to be?". There was a fine line in between " I care so much about the details" to " I don't care" because nothing really mattered after losing Darien. So together my daughters and I gathered as many pictures as we could along with some pictures their Dad's family had and the pictures were used for the video slide and the tables in the funeral parlor. For a second I forgot it was his funeral and I had this thought that he was in another room and would come back in and look at all of the pictures with me

Then I noticed the Memorial cards with his picture on them and the beautiful poem that my daughters and I made up together that expressed the impact my Son had on people and who he was as a person. My mind was racing in slow motion. I remembered thinking that I was very satisfied with the funeral parlor and that everyone there was so nice and helpful. They really made what was happening a little softer on us. As we waited I wondered if enough people were told that he had passed and if everyone was given the right information and address. My daughters went across the street before the first afternoon service started to get something from the store. Their Dad and I waited in the front foyer for them to return. They returned from the store with gum and mints for all of us. At this point so many flowers were being brought in from different people along with some potted plants. In came a very large and beautiful arrangement from his coworkers. I made a mental note to bring most of the flowers to his Memorial site where he had the accident of which his friends set up as a place to honor him, I thought they would look great there, so when the last day of service was over we were bringing them there.

At this point I was still operating in robot mode which kept me from losing it. I was never the type of person that would fall apart on someone and if I let myself go, I think I would have had a heart attack right there. I had to keep myself from having a serious break down.

The first day of the funeral was numbly overwhelming. Our family got there earlier to have some alone time with each other and my Son. I remember walking into the room very aware that it was becoming hard to breathe. As I walked in I was almost afraid to look up front and view his casket. That would make his death officially true to the part of me that was still in denial. I looked around and I saw all of the beautiful flowers on display for the service, so many beautiful flowers. As my eyes got closer to the big red heart that said Love Mom and Dad I knew his coffin was coming into view next and I didn't want to look, not yet. I wanted to avoid seeing him in the coffin. But it was impossible, I could not avoid seeing him there, he looked so still and peaceful, never to move again in a forever endless sleep, this was too much to take in. At this point I walked over to the casket and I had to touch his lips, I had asked them if they could use less embalming on him since he was being cremated, maybe his lips and cheeks could have a softer feel. Usually when someone dies they use so much embalming their lips and face feel cold and hard like rubber. I didn't want my Son to feel like that, he had beautiful lips and such a great smile and I wanted to remember him that way.

There he was in front of me wearing the clothes we took from his closet. It had to be the clothes he normally wore because he loved shopping and picking up new clothes to wear and I knew that whatever he bought for himself he truly enjoyed wearing it. He looked so handsome and sharp. Here was my Son lying in front of me, the stillest moment I would ever have had of him was in this very moment. I felt so sick. I reached down to touch his lips and to my surprise they did feel soft. I remember thinking " if people had batteries, we could just go out and get some new batteries and he would come back to life", But that was not the case in this situation, humans die. I remember missing him so much while he was right there in front of me and it was such a weird feeling. I also thought about the upcoming decision I made on having him cremated and even though my spiritual beliefs in reincarnation are that his Soul will enter a new life and he will have a new body, the human part of me was questioning if maybe I was doing something wrong by having him cremated.

Just the idea of burning someone's body made me revisit my faith and doubt my decision, but just for a moment. A thought entered my mind, "what if he needs his body in his new life and here I am destroying the one he had?" But as I said the thought lasted just a few minutes. I will be cremated myself when the time comes. I don't believe in making people feel guilty over a grave, who visits, who didn't show up, how often do you go?. By this time people started to come in and it felt so awkward as each of them approached me with that distraught sympathy look, afraid that I might lose it on them and start screaming and fall to the ground. Honestly I was afraid that could happen too, but I fought to keep myself contained and hold it together. I believe the situation was awkward for everyone at the funeral, no one knew exactly what to say or how to help. I think it's so much harder for everyone involved when a child dies. It's so unexpected and children are not supposed to die.

His Dad and I were standing together as the people came in and although we were divorced we stood together and accepted condolences from everyone that came to show support and honor my Son. I had to put aside the not so pleasant past between us and try to deal with next couple of hours. Together we lost a Son and there is not another person alive that was feeling what we alone could only feel as his parents. His Dad didn't express much but I knew inside that he was so broken over this tragedy. He also lost his one and only Son. I remember sitting with him looking at the wall with the picture slides.

We just sat there emotionally exhausted trying to make sense out of it all. We listened to a few selected Song on the CD that played along with the pictures and his Dad mentioned really liking the Song " Dancing in the Sky" by Dani and Lizi He asked me a few times what the name of that Song was. There were so many people that showed up that we haven't seen in years and it made me wonder how they found out. I was so glad they came. I couldn't reach everyone as I was in my own world trying to deal with the planning of the funeral. It would have been really great to see all these people under different circumstances, but sometimes it's the only time you see people unfortunately. I found myself wondering if I ordered enough cards for all of the people who showed up. By this time more flowers were being brought into the room and I noticed my daughters were talking with people who were expressing their condolences and I felt so sad that they had to go through this and be in this room listening to people repeatedly telling them how sorry they were for the loss of their brother. I know they were both in a lot of pain, as they loved their brother Darien so much.

They always had a good time together as siblings, he was their older Brother, to them he was supposed to be there always looking out for them, not lying in a casket. They will forever love him and miss him. I am sure that he is watching over them every moment because he loved them greatly too. I never believed in graves and with cremation I now had to pick out urns for family members who were getting some of his ashes. It felt more comforting to give some of his ashes to family members then to put his body in the ground. We also hired a Spiritual Speaker through the funeral parlor to come and speak about Darien's life and who he was as a person. People usually have a Priest ,but I didn't want the usual Service for my Son, I wanted people to freely express themselves and talk about my Son and to talk to each other instead of waiting silently through a Sermon. I didn't want my Son to be another death, I wanted people to share what they felt about him. Even though it was the most painful part of my life everyone's speech and sharing made it so beautiful.

My daughters and I, along with their Dad each made our own speeches and I wrote a few poems of which I read when I spoke of my Son. A few of his friends got up and said some powerful and deep things about Darien, I sat there so amazed that my Son affected all these people so greatly. He was truly loved by so many people. I was very pleased with how the Service turned out and how many people came up to tell us beautiful stories about Darien. I'm sure my Son Darien was there watching everything that was going on during the Service for him and he felt so touched by seeing the love expressed that everyone had for him, as I'm not sure he knew how truly loved and valued he really was.

6. BEFORE THE ACCIDENT

My Son had been in quite a few accidents throughout the years, but he always came away with just a few scratches. In 2013, I happened to be with his Dad at a comedy show of which I was in, and before they called me to go on stage both of our phones kept ringing. So we realized it must be something important and answered the phone. We then found out that our Son was riding his motorcycle and was hit by another motorcycle and was being rushed to the hospital. We jumped up and hurried to the hospital and there was our Son with this little grin on his face as he was saying, "I'm fine, thanks for coming." We found out that he had broken his bone in his lower leg and they would need to brace it with a titanium rod to hold the bone together. I remember thinking to myself, " Okay maybe he will stop riding now."

Every time he went out on his motorcycle I always had a sick feeling that I was going to lose him. Honestly throughout his childhood I had those feelings because my Son had no fear. He had two head on collisions with cars and walked away with just a few scratches. We were parents who were always worried about what he would try next. I gave him all of the Mom talks about how anything could happen. It didn't matter to him because he believed that in order to truly live you had to take chances. He loved the rush, the competition and the stories. We were so stressed and tired of those 1am phone calls and hospital visits, only to see him planning something with more risk involved each time. We were always more worried about him than our daughters, as they never took the risks that my Son did.

When he rented his first and unfortunately last apartment I was still worried, but I didn't have to hear about all of his plans to build the motorcycle faster or what parts he was adding or taking away, or which road he was going to try the bike out on. I was able to sleep a little better because I didn't stay up waiting for him to come home because he lived on his own. After the accident where he broke his leg I thought for sure that he would somehow wake up and maybe see the dangers of riding a motorcycle. I honestly was so happy with the thought of him not riding anymore. That accident left him out of work for over four months. Thank God he had a great job and had saved some money. Although after four months it was running out.

As time passed his leg had healed and he went back to work and eventually took out a loan, (against my wishes) to buy a brand new red Ducati motorcycle. Little did I know back then that this would be the last bike he would ever ride. Soon after he picked up the bike he came to my house and asked me if I had a cross or something religious to pray over and then place inside his motorcycle. I went inside and brought out a light blue and dark blue mixed rosary bead cross necklace. I gave it to him and together we placed it deep inside a space underneath his seat. I always remember that day, I felt honored and sad at the same time. I was glad he thought I could protect him, but I also knew it wasn't realistic. Knowing it made him feel safer definitely made me feel better with the hopes that he would be extra careful while riding.

He loved this new motorcycle it was like a dream come true for him. He always found different ways to alter it to make it lighter and faster. I never understood the obsession, but thinking about it now. It must have felt so freeing to not have fear and cut through the wind like a knife. I myself have fears of speed, heights and anything dangerous. But for someone who doesn't have that fear, they cannot understand the fear the rest of us have. He lived for every adventurous moment. I would always see his posts on Facebook about some new part or road he tried out.

I was never aware of how fast he was *actually* riding. I just always thought it was a little faster than your average rider. I gave him so many lectures on how unsafe it was to ride, but it was not within my control he was not twelve years old anymore. All I could do was remind him to be careful and ride safely. I always hoped he would grow out of this stage of the need for speed. He knew I was not happy about the new bike so he didn't push his "going fast stores" on me. Sometimes he would ride to my house and just stop in and have a cup of tea with me and then meet up with a few friends.

He was always planning rides and "meet ups" with friends and he loved showing them his new accessories and riding gear for the bike. I was not so happy when he bought the GoPro camera for his helmet, as it made me worry that he would take more risks just to capture it on camera. This made me very worried, but I knew my words could never change his mind. I always secretly hoped he would meet a girl that would want to have a serious relationship and distract him from the bike, but that never happened, most of the girls thought it was awesome that he had a motorcycle. I guess when you are young it's considered cool to have a motorcycle.

Sometimes he would stop by and just lay down across my couch and ask me to rub his hair and forehead, he loved affection and had no problem asking for it. It didn't matter that he was older, I still saw him as my little baby. He was so strong on the outside, but yet so soft and vulnerable on the inside. We shared many conversations and he was very open about things that were bothering him. Sometimes he could be very sensitive and get hurt easily. We would always talk about things and then he would say "Thanks Mom" which usually meant he heard my opinion and he will eventually figure it out in his own way.

One thing I am sure of is that I always gave my Son so much love and attention whenever he was around. I gave the same to my daughters, but I think he received a little more attention from me, as I was always trying to over compensate for an indifference he had with his Dad. I had grown up with my brother and father who also had an indifferent relationship and it always broke my heart that my dad did not know how to give love to my brother and that somehow it broke his spirit. So I became determined to never let that happen to my Son. Indifference to me seems so poisonous and I feel it freezes the soul because the misunderstanding is never healed.

I tried to teach my Son to express himself and to talk about his feelings and to fight for what he wanted. I am so proud to see that he developed into an awesome human being with a great personality. Actually I must say that all three of my children turned out like that. They are and will always be the proudest moments of my entire life.

7. THE ACCIDENT

My Son woke up that day just like any other day with the thought of riding his motorcycle, as it was the main thing he loved to do. Earlier that day he saw his girlfriend Natashia and when he left she told him to be careful riding. He wanted to ride with his friends, but everyone was busy. He asked his friend Jon to ride and at first Jon was reluctant, but then decided to go. He didn't want my Son to ride alone. My Son was riding in front of Jon and started to go faster and at one point Jon could no longer see him as they were on a curvy and winding road. Right before Jon finally caught up with him I believe he noticed some sparks or fire up ahead in the sky and then to the right he noticed my Son's body lying on the ground by a big tree.

A Man in a truck had just passed him by and made a U-turn to come back, Jon was standing there in shock emotionally frozen as the man ran over to pull my Son's body away from his motorcycle which was in pieces and went up in flames. It was so devastating for Jon to see his good friend (my Son) lying there motionless. To this day I thank God for that man because if he didn't pull him away we would not have been able to have an open casket for the two nights of service before the cremation.

We believe my Son's bike hit a bump in the road and then hydroplaned into a tree and was then thrown further along. Both my Son and his friend's helmet had cameras on them. The police had my Son's camera and when we went there his camera showed all the footage up until the actual accident and then it cut out. Thank God, I wouldn't have been able to see that. In my mind I had this day dream of the accident and I saw my Son say, " Oh, Fuck." Right before he went into the tree.

Two weeks later we had all gone to see a Medium and the Medium said that my Son hit something solid and right before he struck the solid structure my Son said "Oh Fuck." I know now for sure that my Son knew in that moment that there was no going back and that his last accident would be in that moment and that his life would be taken. When I think about him knowing that it was the end it just crushes my heart, it makes me wonder if he was scared even if only for a few seconds. To this day at around 8pm on the 24th of July my mind replays his moment of impact and it always makes me wonder if he was afraid and knew that was his last day on earth.

It kills me to think that for even a brief moment he was in *pain.* As a Mother I *could* not ever imagine my child in pain the thought alone gives me instant anxiety. I can't even go there mentally it makes my hairs stand up. Even as a child I couldn't even take a tear falling from his eyes. I was so attached to his being happy. He was my squeaky wheel and he always spoke up when something bothered him. So I always tried to fix whatever made him unhappy. Whenever I think of him I miss him so much it's so hard to face the fact that I will never see him again on earth.

I know I will see him when it's my turn to leave here but I would rather have him right now and be able to hear his voice and see him laugh and smile. He had such a beautiful smile. I loved that smile as it was so contagious. Even if I was mad at him he could find a way to make me smile.

8.   PRECIOUS MEMORIES

The memories that run through my head can be very random as I remember giving him a bath in his little tub in the kitchen sink and when I turned on the water it made this loud noise and his eyes got so big and shocked looking. I remember having to wean him off the bottle only to find him secretly stealing his sister's bottle. I remember how he used to use a baby voice even at an older age to get me to give in to him and it worked every time. He learned to play piano at an early age, he had only two lessons and he knew how to play a full Song. The piano teacher said there was a recital coming up and that he was really good, but that it may be too soon. He told her that he wanted to do it so she let him come to the recital and when he arrived he forgot his sheet music, the teacher was nervous, but she let him go on stage anyway. He went up to the piano, looked at the audience and played his Song perfectly.

He was always trying to create something, once he was a little older and he needed a razor blade to cut through some material so we made him put a board underneath it to keep from cutting his leg. He got up to use the bathroom and when he came back he was so caught up in what he was doing he forgot to put the board back and he ended up cutting right though the middle of his thigh. There went another trip to the hospital in which he needed many inner and outer stitches. Another time he pulled his shirt down over his knees to his ankles pretending to be a Pac Man, and he when he tried to jump up he got stuck and fell straight down on our slate steps. "Back to the hospital again", we were lucky they knew we were good parents and that he kept getting hurt because he was so hyper and his mind was constantly creating new ideas.

I was more of the disciplining parent when it came to safety, I was so afraid of my children doing anything close to risky. Their Dad would take them to steep hills on the side of the parkway and let them slide down the snow in sleighs, one day I went with them and I watched my daughter Dakota Rose slide down the hill and then go up in the air and then just drop into some ditch, my heart was in my hand. Thank God I missed all the previous trips. I would have never let them go again. I think it's a "male thing" they don't seem to fuss or worry as much as most Mothers do. So being the disciplining parent, it also makes you the "not so much fun parent", that's okay my job was to keep them from the hospital.

I will always remember the first time my Son felt hurt over a girl, he liked this girl but she liked another boy, it took weeks for him to be himself again. He was so heartbroken. Then many years later he met the first girl our whole family fell in love with, her name was Christine. He met her while he started college and they were in the same class. She had such a great family and my Son fit himself right in. She had a Step Dad George that my Son really looked up to and admired. I remember Christine and my Son Darien were so in love, they were so cute together. It was the first time my Son was dating someone that he felt was in his corner no matter what. And of course having so much attention made him feel so sure that he could do anything and she would always be there.

I was so happy that this whole new family loved my Son, they had a healthy family life and they always included my Son in everything they did. Her Mom loved my Son as if he was her Son and I loved her daughter Christine as if she were my daughter. Sometimes when I would look at pictures of my Son the memories would rush in and take over my thoughts. My thoughts could range from extreme sadness to a feeling of pride in knowing that he was my Son. I then remember the exact moment in the picture and it takes me back to all of the different looks his face made, and his big sparkly brown eyes which were for the most part always happy and enthusiastic looking. I can remember every expression on his face, the curve of his cheekbones, his voice and his laughter. Then if I stare at the picture for a while I remember that there is no life left in the picture , and that only the memory of it brings it back to life. Then I begin to feel sad that it's just a picture.

I'm good for a few hours and then all I need is one thing to remind me of him and I'm thrown back into this repetitive cycle of being happy to remember and sad that it's only a memory now. I have an area in my house with most of his belongings, it's starting to look like a little shrine. I cannot let those things go, they are the very essence of what holds me together. Every morning I awake to say my good morning to him. I feel it brings me some comfort in knowing that parts of him are still around.

I had also had a tattoo of his face put on my forearm and I had the tattoo artist put some of my Son's ashes into the ink, that way I will always feel like a part of him is with me. My older daughter Danelle had his signature tattooed on her arm and another tattoo on her back with the words, " In Life and Death you've always stole my Heart". My youngest daughter Dakota Rose has a small Shrine under the TV stand with his picture, shoes, watches, and other belongings, she even kept his mattress and sleeps on it every night.

·   And his Dad had a tattoo on his forearm with our Son's name and date. These things and rituals somehow help give meaning to our loss.

By this point my Son was into cars and drifting, he would go to Englishtown, New Jersey to drift because they had a track there. I believe some people were helping him buy new tires as the old ones would burn out from the drifting, or maybe that's what he told me. His very first "New Car" was a Nissan and I remember he could not get a loan and I was not in a position to cosign, we were at the dealer and they could not give him a loan and he was so disappointed. He was talking with his girlfriend's step Dad George on the phone and George decided to loan the full amount of the car to my Son and he said he would set up a payment plan for my Son to pay him back.

Within a short time the money was wired to the dealership. I was in shock and happy at the same time for my Son. Oh the smile on my Son's face in that moment, I wish George could have actually been there to see the self esteem and value he just gave my Son. Unfortunately the car became another hobby that propelled my Son into faster speed and more challenges down the road. I just saw a car, but my Son saw an open road, his first car accident involved him sliding head on into a tree because his tires were so bald from the drifting I guess he lost control of the car. The car was totaled and yet my Son walked away with a few scratches and airbag burns, thank God. My Son at this point was becoming more obsessed and involved with his cars and drifting and less involved with having a girlfriend. I was so broken hearted to see the changes in their relationship. I had hoped that Christine was going to marry my Son one day. I guess all things change.

My Son had a great job with the Ironworkers union, he was a shop steward of the freedom towers and was making great money and on the weekends he rode his motorcycle which was probably where his great money was going. He was always buying new parts and tires etc. Again I was not happy with the motorcycle part of his life and there was not much I could do about it. So I minded my business when I felt the urge to say something.

By this time he was officially no longer seeing Christine and we were all sad about this, I honestly feel she was the best thing that ever happened to him, but the timing was off. Maybe if he was a little older and met her then, I'm sure it would have worked out better. But this is life and it's all part of growing and learning who we are as we mature. To this day I make sure I keep in touch with her. She will always be my other daughter. Her soul is so beautiful and she is the kindest person I know.

I remember when my Son took over the garage and he built shelves and he put a speaker system in there and then bolted the garage shut and went out. About 3am the music went off in the garage really loud and I could not get in touch with him. When he finally called me back most of my neighbors were awake from the music. He then said to me, "don't worry just cut the lock off." Then I realized that all of the tools were in the garage and I had nothing to cut it with. He never looked at things as being complicated. His solutions sounded so easy but harder in reality.

So I asked a neighbor if they could cut the lock off at about 5am. Well, I guess my Son figured they were up anyway from the loud music. He was growing up and it was time for his first apartment. He found a cute basement apartment in Bayshore L.I. I was so proud of him and although I missed him, he needed his own space. He enjoyed buying furniture for the apartment and decorating it. I loved watching him create his own style in the apartment.

9. SURVIVNG HOLIDAYS AND GATHERINGS

It's almost 2016 and I cannot believe how fast the year went by because of the pain and emptiness of losing my Son was still as strong as ever, if not even more intense. Although I am thankful to have all of the memories with my Son from the past 26 years I still would much rather have a whole future with him which is now missing. Thank God I have a very vivid memory and I can remember specific moments down to what was said in conversations with my Son. I can even remember his exact voice in my head and all of the expressions he made on his face. I can replay them in my mind and relive those moments and allow all of the good feelings to rush in.

I can remember coming across a Mother's Day Card that he had made for me and when I read the part where he wrote, " I'll always be there for you" I remembered thinking to myself, "It's not true, he cannot be there for me, he lied. " and sometimes I feel that when he watches me read the card and he notices me staring at that particular part, that he feels sad and wishes he could be here to say "It's alright Mom I'm okay."

For Thanksgiving I stayed in Florida and went to my Aunt's house which was nice but my head was somewhere else. I really didn't feel so thankful, as I could not find the good in anything at that point I just wanted to be with my three children and celebrate being thankful with them. The Holiday dynamics were now changing, we were now so aware of his missing place setting at the table. For Christmas we went to his memorial site and decorated it with red flowers and balloons and lights and we just went home. My daughters had a few things to do but the spirit of Christmas was just not there that first Christmas.

The First New Years Eve. I was in New York for New Years Eve and I had no desire to celebrate in any way. I remember my girlfriend Laura and her husband Jim were going out for new Years and asked me to come with them. I thanked them for the offer, but decided to stay in my room. There was no way that I could have been around so many happy people while my heart was just ripped out. I went into my daughter Dakota Rose's room, as she had been living with my girlfriend Laura and I put on the TV, then a few minutes before midnight I held some of my Son's memories, his picture, his helmet and his watch and I talked to him and I told him I wasn't happy that he wasn't there for New Years and that I missed him.

I actually put his helmet over my head as if in some way I would be able to feel his presence. I even sprayed the room with his cologne so that I could close my eyes and pretend he was in the room with me. I never cry but I was crying now. He was my little man, my baby and he was gone. I had so many dreams about how things would be when he got older. I couldn't wait for the day that I would watch him as a father with his children. I knew for sure that he was going to be a very interesting Father who would always make sure that everyone had fun. My daughters used to say that when they had children Darien was going to be the daredevil uncle with the crazy fun ideas. Now they have to tell their children that there was an uncle they will never meet. They would have loved their uncle Darien.

New Years Eve. I found New Years Eve to be really hard. I felt like there was no reason to celebrate a New Year. It just made losing my Son feel so much further away. Soon I will be saying I lost my Son last year. I didn't want it to be a whole year when it was just about five months since he passed. I wanted it to still feel as if I just saw him. Everyone around me seemed so happy and I couldn't deal with that. I wasn't jealous that they had their happy moments, I just couldn't join them and at that moment it felt like I would never be able to. I felt so scared to go anywhere without my Son. It felt like the suffering made me feel as if I was honoring the life that he lived and I wanted so desperately to make sure he was never forgotten.

New Years is that time when people create do-overs and make resolutions so they feel refreshed with a new outlook towards tomorrow. I had none of those feelings because my tomorrows were going to be very different without my Son. It doesn't matter if you have other children, each one is so perfectly and individually different. No child could ever be replaced and they are all so unique in their personalities. My Son didn't hold back when something was bothering him, he loved loud and he complained loud. It's one of the things I loved so much about him, he had a very strong personality and yet he could be so very vulnerable at the same time. He always found a way to demand my attention and my heart always went out to him.

Now it's the New Year and the Holiday is Valentine's Day, the international sweetheart day. I was his first sweetheart, he loved making me gifts for Valentine's Day or buying me them from the school cafeteria Holiday sale. The look on his face was always priceless when he watched me open one of his gifts. I know he couldn't wait for the chocolate heart that I had bought him, but he always waited long enough to first see the big smile on my face when I opened his gift first. He was so proud of himself. When Valentine's Day came I still bought him a chocolate heart, a card and a red heart balloon that I sent up into the sky later that night wishing him love and happiness and whispering an " I Love You" to him.

Easter came and it felt weird because the Easter before was the last time we were all together at our house in Seaford. My children usually showed up a little late, Darien came even later. But we were together and had fun telling stores. Now this was the first Easter where I no longer had a house or Son and my daughters no longer had their house or their brother. Selling my house, moving and losing my Son almost killed me.

Mother's Day was the worst, I was now missing a child and it stood out *so much* on Mother's Day. I remember my Daughter's Dakota Rose, Danelle and her fiancé Adam took me out to eat and bought me beautiful gifts, spiritual gifts. We had a good time but it was so sad without Darien being there. Life had begun to change for all of us, as we now had to do things in a different way.

In a few months my daughter Danelle and her fiancé Adam will be getting married, I went with my daughter, her sister Dakota Rose and their dad to help Danelle look for a wedding dress, (God my Son would have loved to see her picking out a dress). She looked beautiful in every one she tried on. She ended up finally picking one out by a designer named (Dakota) which was her sister's name.

She was having a Barn wedding in a really nice place in Loydd Harbor in Huntington L.I. New York. We all helped her as much as we could with decorating the barn and getting things ready. When it was finished it looked so beautiful, I was so proud of her and Adam for making their wedding exactly the way they planned it in their head, it was so "them".

Both my daughters were so creative with planning it out. Every time we came up with an idea there was that feeling to call my Son and tell him what was going on because that's what we usually did. But now he would never be on the other end of the phone. But it didn't take away the automatic impulse to reach out to him. He was always interested in what his sisters were up to and what their plans were and I know he was excited about his sister Danelle getting married to Adam soon. I know for sure that he was happy for them. It was an occasion that he was really looking forward to attending.

As my daughter Danelle's wedding date was approaching I was so excited yet so sad. My Son did everything with us and now he was not going to be there. It brought me back to a conversation that I had with him about giving her a wedding gift. He came to my house and asked me what I thought about him giving her $1000 for her wedding. His face was so lit up because he knew it was a lot to give but he really wanted to give her a great gift and he was excited about it. I must say that when he said "$1000" I also thought it was a really nice gift. And I realized that it was a very big gift to him because he was always buying new parts for his motorcycle and never seemed to have any money left.

I felt so proud of him in that moment because he showed me that he loved his sister so much that he put her happiness ahead of his own. He felt that it was more important she have the extra money towards her future. It was so hard for me to not tell anyone that I had the conversation with him about what he planned to give her as a gift, as it made me so happy that I wanted to tell the world that I had such a great Son and that he wanted to put his sister's happiness and future ahead of his own. Whenever I see my children loving each other and being kind to each other on their own, my heart just melts and it reminds me that my children turned out to be really beautiful inside and out. I'm so proud of all three of them, they are my life and my love of life.

Danelle and Adam's wedding was really awesome. My daughter Danelle looked so beautiful in her dress and Adam looked so handsome. They made such a beautiful couple. The food was delicious and the music was great everything was so good except for my Son not being there to enjoy it with us. I strongly believe that he was there watching the whole thing and feeling happy for them both. While also wishing he could be there physically to stand next to his sister and walk her down the aisle. Danelle and Adam made a special table for Darien with some of his personal items on it, we also had a lot of his pictures, I'm sure he was happy about that. I'm glad that we were able to enjoy the wedding and at the same time honor the memory of my Son. He was in all of our hearts throughout the evening, and I know that it was hard for my daughter-knowing that her brother couldn't be there to share such a beautiful moment in her life.

Christmas was here and I flew into New York to be with my daughter's for the holidays. Danelle and Adam invited me and my daughter Dakota Rose over to have dinner with them. They made a great dinner and later we each opened our gifts. The gifts were great *but I was happier that we were able to celebrate in the spirit of family.* Everything worked out well, I had brought some balloons for my Son to send up into the sky for Christmas for him, and we ended up doing that later on. I was so glad to be with both of my daughters, as I cannot imagine life without them . They are so beautiful and smart and I am so proud to have them as my daughters and in my life. They miss their brother so much and they miss hearing his stories, *and he was always great with his stories.* He was packed with personality and always captured our attention. I thank God every day that my children turned out to be really great human beings, they are a delight to be around and are always kind to people and respectful of others. They don't have a mean bone in their body. My Son was greatly missed at my daughter's wedding by everyone there. When we started to take pictures, I felt as if we were supposed to go find him and tell him that we needed him to stand next to us and smile for the pictures. He was supposed to be standing next to us and included in the family pictures. I know he was definitely there in spirit, as I know my Son was so strong willed that he would probably fight an Angel in Heaven to be there. So I leave it in my mind the picture of him being right there next to Danelle as she walked down the aisle.

10. RECIEVING BEAUTIFUL SIGNS

For my Son's One Year Anniversary I had my daughter Dakota Rose make me a CD of songs that helped me feel I was not alone with my pain and that someone else out there understood what I was feeling. It was so nice to see many of his friends come to the memorial. Many of them parked their cars up and down the street. One of his friends let me use his car to play the CD through his speakers. I had picked about eleven songs and knew each one. After the memorial I went back to Florida to my condo and I had my computer on and the screen wallpaper on the computer was a picture of all three of my children. I was sitting there looking at their picture while playing the CD and I started to cry and out of nowhere a song came on that I didn't recognize.

The words were so beautiful and exactly what I needed to hear, only they sounded as if my Son were saying them to me because in that moment I was falling apart. I had to call my daughter to ask her when she put that song on the CD and she said she didn't, she doesn't even know the song. I truly believe that it was a sign from my Son Darien letting me know he saw me falling apart and through the song he was trying to comfort me. The song is by Rascal Flatts... Here are the words:

Lori Grasman

I Won't Let Go

It's like a storm that cuts a path, it breaks your will, it feels like that

You think you're lost, but you're not lost on your own, you're not alone

I will stand by you, I will help you through, when you've done all you

can do, if you can't cope. I will dry your eyes, I will fight your fight, I

will hold you tight and I won't let go it hurts my heart, to see you cry, I

know it's dark, this part of life. Oh it finds us all (finds us all) and

we're too small to stop the rain, oh but when it rains I will stand by

you, I will help you through, when you've done all you can do and you

can't cope. I will dry your eyes, I will fight your fight, I will hold you

tight, and I won't let you fall. Don't be afraid to fall, I'm right here to

catch you. I won't let you down, it won't let you down. You're gonna

make it, yeah I know you can make it, cause I will stand by you, I will

help you through When you've done all you can do and you can't cope,

I will dry your eyes, I will fight your fight. I will hold you tight and I

won't let go, Oh I'm gonna hold you and I won't let go No I Won't.

Signs

From early on after my Son Darien passed I have received many signs from him. These signs have helped me feel more comfortable in knowing that he is okay. In the beginning I would leave my condo only to come home and find my dining room lights on with the ceiling fan moving on the highest speed. For almost two months this kept happening and I even had someone check out my electric for any shorts in the wires and there were none. One day I decided to try free writing by holding a pen with just the weight of my hand on the pen with my eyes closed and on two separate occasions the word (Love) was written upside down, almost as if he were sitting in front of me facing me.

A Medium had told me that my Son wanted me to be careful and slow down and during a trip to New York by car with my daughter Dakota Rose and I happened to get a call from my Son's girlfriend, (Natashia), telling me that she had went to a Medium also and that the Medium said that my Son kept saying the number twenty, or something with the number twenty and so I told Natashia that my birthday was in a few days and it was March 20. As she was telling me this we heard police sirens, I had no idea they were for me so I kept driving, eventually we were forced to pull over by a policeman and I asked him why he had pulled me over and he said I was speeding and that he was from the "Darien Police Department" in Darien Georgia and that I was going over 90 miles an hour, I told him there was no way I was going that fast and I never drive fast.

When I realized that he said " Darien Police Dept. and Darien, GA." I then told the police officer that my Son made him stop me because I was probably going to have an accident and that it was no coincidence that I was pulled over and that my Son had just passed away and that his name was Darien. I think at first the officer thought I was crazy and he was very determined to give me a ticket, but he came back to my car and gave me a sad kind of smile and then asked me to drive safer and to have a good day. I seriously had no idea I was going so fast that I put my car on cruise control for the rest of the trip.

Another Medium from Russia had told me that my Son had been giving me so many signs and that he will send me another one and that it will be outside this time. Later that night I was walking through my development while on the phone with my girlfriend who had just had breast cancer surgery and while we were talking, my daughter Danelle's upcoming wedding came into the conversation and I remember telling my friend that it was killing me that my Son wouldn't be there at the wedding and in that second I looked down at the street and there was an old silver necklace with a small army tag type of pendant and when I picked it up and looked at it in the light it said "the best" in small letters with a small heart and above it in much larger letters it said " I'LL BE THERE". I had tears in my eyes and I believe my friend did too when I told her what it said.

What are the chances that as soon as I say he won't be there I find an army tag pendant saying "I'll be There" right at my feet in the dark and on the street. I will say that was one of the most beautiful signs so far, I feel that my Son found a way to make sure I knew he would be there no matter what. It was such an awesome sign.

One day I was very upset and crying while I was driving away from my condo and something made me look back and up at the sky, there above me was a huge angel shaped cloud bending over my building facing me as if it were about to swoop down and hug me. Another time I found a dime and penny outside my car door as I was getting out and I noticed one was the year he was born and the other was the year he passed.

The night that his grandfather had passed I had this dream where everyone in our family was there except for his grandfather, we seemed to be at a party and in the dream my Son was younger and he seemed real happy and somewhat secretive. He was standing by this room with colored lights and music and so I asked him what he was doing and he said, " I have to go in there now and dance Mom." I remember wondering after that dream where his grandfather was, only to find out that while I was having that dream, at the same moment his grandfather passed away in the hospital. It was as if he already knew in the dream that he would soon be seeing his grandfather.

I was driving again and while I felt so distraught and really losing it I pulled over and turned on the radio and at that exact moment a song that reminds me of him came on at the part where it says, " I swear it will get easier", I know that was him as most of the signs he sends me are when I'm really down. I find that signs help us put things into perspective and remind us that they are safe and with God. For me they bring me comfort in remembering his existence and all the love that we shared along with all of the experiences we shared as a family. Nothing could ever take that away. Thank God for memories.

My daughter Dakota Rose also received a sign while she stopped to get gas, she noticed this large beautiful rose growing among some weeds in a patch of dirt by the side of the gas station and she thought the rose looked so perfect and yet familiar and she pulled it right out of the ground and took it with her. When she got home she realized the rose looked exactly like the rose that was in Darien's Prayer card, from the petals to the stem and leaves, they were all in the exact same place, even the color was the same bright red shade. She now has it saved in a book. I know it was my Son's way of telling her that he was fine.

I remember one day lying by my pool listening to music and feeling sad because a song I had listened to reminded me of Darien. I was leaning back with my eyes closed and when I opened them there was a huge very white heart shaped cloud over me in the sky. Where I am in Florida, the clouds are three dimensional looking and that heart shaped cloud was such a beautiful sight to see when I opened my eyes.

My daughter Danelle was sent a sign from Darien when she went to work at the waitress job and she approached a table where a boy looked just like her brother Darien, he was sitting with his family and my daughter looked at this boy and started crying so much she had to leave the table and walk away. She went back to the table and his parents asked her why she was upset and she said, "I'm sorry, he looks just like my brother who just passed away." Then the boy's mother started to cry for my daughter's loss. Then that very same night a little later on after gaining her composure she attended another table only to find our old neighbors sitting at the table, at first she did not recognize them until they started to tell her who they were. They asked her how our family was doing and the she told them that her brother recently passed. Sometimes signs come through by forcing us to face a memory and remind us of our loss.

11. OBSESSIVE THOUGHTS AND FEELINGS

My thoughts were so scattered after losing my Son and there was so much emotional pain. There were a few times when I became obsessed with feeling I could not go on living without my Son. One night the feeling was so strong that I almost lost the ability to see beyond the moment. I could not sleep and as I was lying there dwelling on how exhausting the pain was from losing my Son, I had no will left to do anything. So for about four hours I started to convince myself that I couldn't deal with it all and I just wanted to be with my Son. My mind began to justify my leaving this world and I started to convince myself that all of the pain would go away once I was gone.

During my obsessive thinking I was startled by the sound of my Son's voice in my head, which was so resonating and loud as he said, "Why don't you practice what you preach about your belief in reincarnation and look up what would happen if you took your life." I then sat up in bed and went on my ipad to look it up and there it was as bright as daylight. It explained that if I were to end my life before I was originally supposed to die, I would remain in a state of limbo until my actual earthly date and during that time the main thing I would see over and over again would be who found my body, my funeral, my children and my family.

I would then have to face watching how taking my life had hurt them and how it affected their lives, and by taking my life it affects those close to me in negative ways and it hurts them to the point where their lives are forever changed because of my death, then I would also have to take on that karma. I would be held responsible for any detours in life made upon those who were very affected by my choosing to leave.

Our life is a gift and we are just not supposed to give up, it's like telling God that we don't accept or want his gift. After reading a little more I realized I could never and would never take my life, because I would never want to hurt my daughters in that way. They were filled with so much pain from losing their brother that to lose me too would crush them emotionally, and what would happen if we all just gave up because we felt broken and lost. God wants us to survive all of life's experiences that come our way no matter how tough they can be.

So at around 5:30 am I took a deep breath in and looked up at the ceiling and thanked my Son for being in my head and telling me to find out how things work in terms of the responsibility of our Soul. I knew in that moment my only choice was to go to sleep and let the coming days help bring my emotions and thoughts to a better place.

My Personal Ups and Downs

On a good day I was strong and dealing on some level with the loss, then ten minutes later I was falling apart and obsessing over the tragedy. I could go from being with a group of people to wanting to get out of there and race home as quickly as I could. On most days I was just numb and going through the motions and barely functioning. My heart would race and it felt like it was a struggle to breathe. On *really* bad days I felt *annoyed* with people. If they said something that I didn't like I was ready to go into defense mode and snap at them. On good days I could listen to a song and share a sweet memory, on a bad day that very same song killed me inside.

I tried to do what I could to help my daughters get though losing their brother. One daughter could not even talk about it. For me I needed to talk about it. I loved to speak his name and tell stories about him, who he was, what he did and how loving and smart he was. Some people enjoyed listening and others looked as if they felt uncomfortable. I didn't care this was my Son and my life that was shattered so quickly. I felt if I stopped talking about him, that it would make me forget him, and my biggest fear was forgetting him. I would rather be hurt every day then to think he was ever out of my mind. His life mattered and it always will.

People who have not lost a child do not understand that it's all we have left, the memories and pictures. I was so glad there were many videos of him playing guitar and singing. When I watch them its as if I get to see him come to life and in my mind he is alive in that moment. His beautiful voice will never be forgotten. God how the memories flood my mind, 26 years of memories, so many moments all gathered into a mental collage.

Thoughts and Memories

After losing my Son Darien I have noticed that every once in a while I run into a situation where I actually see someone that looks just like my Son, sometimes they have his face, his smile, his haircut or his eyes, he had those beautiful big brown eyes. One time it was his complete look. There was a guy (Cal Morris) playing a violin to the "Prayer" and the expression on his face and every smile and movement that he made had me feeling as if my Son's soul was using that guy's body to remind me that he is in a good place and he is safe and happy and will always remember us. I must tell you that while it was a bit overwhelming it was just as much beautiful because in that moment I got to see my Son alive in the body of this guy who could have been his twin.

Sometimes when I look at pictures they become a sad reminded that I will never know what my so Darien was going to look like when he was 30, 40, 50 years old. He will forever be stuck in my mind in the way he looked when he passed at 26 years old. His beautiful voice will never change in my mind. I once went into a Wendy's and believe it or not I noticed a black kid that had my Son's shape face and eyes sitting at a table. I was going to go home with my chicken pieces, but instead I sat down across from this kid and stared at him while a few tears rolled down my face. It felt kind of strange and yet emotionally beautiful.

Memories

Sometimes I will pass someone who reminds me of my Son and I just stand there and absorb all the memories. Someone's profile, their eyes the way they eat or stand or walk. I went into a Deli and the man behind the counter looked like my Son, it took me by surprise so much that I had to walk away at first. I was afraid that I would just stand there and stare at him. During times like that I try to look at it in a positive way and find the joy in seeing my Son's looks or personality in someone else even if only for a brief moment. I start to think of all the positive and funny times we shared together as Mother and Son.

I realized that by doing that, I don't get pulled into " This is the worst thing in the world that happened to me frame of mind." As a Mother I will never forget my Son and his existence and all that he has contributed to my life, to all our lives. I will say again " The pain never goes away, but I am learning to live with it along with the emptiness of not having him in my life that slips its way into my thoughts." They come and go like waves.

I have two beautiful daughters who I love so much and not one of my children could ever replace the other, because each one is so unique and pulls my heart in a different way at different times. Sometimes I talk to my Son as if he were standing right next to me and I make sure he knows he will always be loved. I enjoy my daughters and all that they are and have become. Through all of this we have become closer and even more loving to each other.

Thy Will Be Done

These three words " Thy Will Be Done" found their way into the most humble part of me that I wasn't aware I had. I found that I could not be angry with God, I was just drained and extremely weak. I had hit bottom with my Son's death, I had NO words, for me time was suspended and everything put me into a state of shock. When I thought of God all I could think of were all the parents before me who have lost their children. I remember when it was someone else's story about child loss I felt so sad for them, I too thought I knew what they were feeling because I had children and I was a Mother, but for me two hours later life went on, I was doing laundry or eating dinner with my family, their pain was not absorbed into my head. But when it happened to me, only then did I realize how bad they were suffering. Being a Mother did not give me the ability to say I knew what they were feeling.

To me my Son's death was something I now had to face and so my faith was being tested in order for me to practice what I believe in. And this meant not blaming God and to believe that my Son had a higher purpose somewhere else. His time here was done and there was nothing I could do to change that. I truly believe that my Son came here to fill a purpose in each of our lives and to leave us with the memory and growth of how he affected our lives with his being in our life. He was an inspiration to many as they watched him being so dedicated with passion towards anything that he did. His good friend Shawn had recently shared with me that his last conversation with my Son was with my Son telling him that he did so much with his life and that he has accomplished more than most people who were much older than him and that he was happy and fulfilled. He also said that most people never live at all.

Losing a child was a very traumatic and life altering experience. For those of you on this road the life you once knew will change. You will change and so will the people around you. I honestly believe that unless someone has lost a child, they have no idea what goes on inside of us mentally, emotionally and physically. People that still have all their children think that being a parent allows them to feel the loss we feel and we are going through. But I will tell you until they are in the same exact situation they cannot relate. Let them keep their opinions to themselves because they cannot even understand 1% of this disturbing torture or the agony of never seeing their child again, it's so permanent.

In the beginning there was so much denial, I kept thinking it was just a bad dream and that I would wake up and my Son would still be here, I had to plan his funeral on auto pilot while keeping an, " I'm alright" look on my face so that my daughters wouldn't fall apart even more than they already did. I survived not being angry at God, I didn't blame him for taking my Son, I wished I could, but I'm more spiritual than that. I am a true believer that things happen for a reason and that we meet people for a reason.

Spiritually my feeling is that God allowed me to have my precious Son for as long as I did until he was ready to take him back. I am so grateful for the time that I did have with my Son even though he is gone and I would rather suffer this pain than to never have known him at all.

And through all of this I am learning a lot about myself and how I handle things. There are areas where I thought I was so tough and could hold anything together, but this brought me to my knees, my baby is gone.

God Bless This Devastating Road

There are no rules in mourning, when you lose a child nothing is set in stone as to how we should act or relate to other. But unless you have lost a child the mourning could not compare to any other loss in the world. Being a parent and realizing that all of your plans and dreams for that child will never happen sends a knife right through your heart. Watching my Son grow from a baby into an adult was amazing, I watched him become a beautiful human being. I watched him as he touched the lives of others, his kindness and his heartaches.

When I see a boy with a beautiful smile it makes me remember his smile through them. It's so hard to go through this while you see the rest of the world has their family all together. The things that used to make me happy don't work anymore. I somehow lost who I am and it's so confusing and I'm not even sure who I want to be. I try to find peace and all that comes through is more anxiety. Decisions became hard to make, as anything that seemed final, brought me more fear and I find I couldn't commit to anything.

There are so many times I wished I wasn't here, but then I get a grip on things and realize, "It's just life." Not everyone is going to get old. I would rather it have been me so that he could have had a longer life and get married one day and have children, but God had different plans. The only thing I pray for now is that I definitely pass before my two daughters, as I could never go through this again, " EVER".

It's funny how some people assume that if you have other children it will be easier for you to move on. For me, my daughters are always a constant reminder that I am missing my Son. But I must admit I am grateful that I have other children. God bless anyone that has lost their only child, I cannot even imagine. Especially for someone who had a child that was murdered. God bless you.

Throughout this grieving process I have so many other parents who have lost children, we relate to each other very well, as we truly understand each other. Together we support each other and are there to help each other during any really bad days. The pain comes and goes and just when you think you are fine another wave of pain shows up and knocks you down. I had lost the feeling to get dressed up and I became very relaxed being home and alone. The only part of me that never shut down was my brain. The thoughts and memories flooded every part of my day and even if I wanted to I couldn't tune them out.

Then there were the forever sleepless nights. I was stressed out an alone living in another state. I tried so hard to fall asleep but I just couldn't there were so many things going through my mind. I was worried about my daughters and I wasn't sure where I should be living. The thought of moving again might kill me this time. They say those three things that can kill you: Divorce, Moving and Death. Well I've had all three, after my divorce I sold my house in New York and right before I moved to Florida my cat Shadow of 15 years died, then my Uncle Tony passed, then two months after I moved to Florida my Son passed, then my Uncle Georgie, my Uncle Andre, my friend Margie's Daughter Rebecca, and my friend Frank Died, in less than a year seven people died, God Bless Them all.

12. STAGES OF GRIEF & THINGS PEOPLE SAY

Denial... Although I thought I was handling things, I was really in some sort of robotic mode which numbed my pain because I could not deal with the impact of what just happened to my Son. So I forced an "I have it all together" look on my face and did what I had to do next. Falling apart was not an option, as a child I couldn't fall apart, my parents were always falling apart and in turn it plunged me right into the role of the caretaker. It's all I know.

Guilt.... I didn't feel guilty as if I did something wrong, but many thoughts went through my head asking myself if I could have done something different. If I didn't sell my house would he still be alive? If I didn't move maybe I would have been with him that day and he wouldn't have been in the accident. My thoughts went as far as, " I should have paid someone to break his motorcycle so he couldn't ride it." But the truth is nothing would have changed God's decision to take him home.

Anger......... I had no anger towards God, and I didn't blame God. I found myself sometimes a little angry at my Son for being so unaware and feeling so free to take risks. He was supposed to stay here and create a whole life and have a family and go to my funeral one day.

Depression.... All I know is that my Son's death changed me, my personality for the most part was always positive and upbeat, I was an outgoing type of person and maybe somewhat hyper. But after losing Darien I couldn't work, didn't want to go out, slept many hours and pretty much stayed home by myself. I didn't want to be around people. I only wanted to be near my daughters. In my mind they were all I had left. And in those moments I had wished I never left my house in Seaford.

Regret.... The only regret I have is that I wished I would have stayed another two weeks in New York after my daughter Danelle's engagement party. I would have been able to be there when he was rushed to the hospital and hold him and to say goodbye. And I would have made sure his Dad was notified even if I had to pay someone to pick him up. He was in a bad situation, but he still deserved to be there while Our Son was dying.

Anxiety...... The anxiety was and is the worst because one moment I was breathing fine and the next moment I could hardly breathe. Out of nowhere my heart would race. Or I could be at the store and I would start to feel nervous or fearful and have to go back home.

Reflection.... Looking back I realize that my Son loved his hobbies with such an intense passion. He couldn't wait to finish work and go home to ride his motorcycle. He studied all there was to know about motorcycles and he was obsessed with the mechanics of it. He had all the types of riding gear available and being cautious he always wore all of the necessary clothing and boots.

He just didn't have that signal that says, " something can happen" and whatever he did, he had no thought that it could not be done. Although having no fear is like a rush to some people there is also a downfall to it. Unfortunately we cannot follow our children around all of the time and lecture them or take away their inspiration for hobbies.

They say some people bargain with God when they lose a loved one, for me I never tried to bargain, I knew there was no miracle that God would let him come back. Being spiritual I also believe in reincarnation, so I believe that my Son's time here was completed, that he gave to those the experience of him and he received from us the experience of us. I also believe that in another life we will have another family (human) experience once again, only we will take on different roles in the family. There is a part of me that thinks that in another life my Son was (my parent) and that I too died at a young age, and so now in this life (my losing him) gives me the experience that he went through when he lost me and that in other lives to come both of us will never lose another child because we have already had that experience.

These are my own beliefs and they have helped me accept that God is always in control every second of the day, as our lives can and will change at any moment. I don't always agree with what God allows or does but I do respect that he has the ultimate perfect reason and that anything that he does or allows is always for our higher purpose. Being human I am beside myself over the loss of my Son, I miss his smile, his voice, his laughter, his whole being and personality, he was and is and will always be so beautiful to me. Remembering God and the purpose of life gently softens the pain, (sometimes) but then sometimes (I will not lie) those moments come and my "spirituality" flies right out the door.

Shocking Things People Say After You Have Lost A Child

I remember someone telling me "I'm sorry for your loss, I lost my uncle and a guy I used to work with." And I remember thinking " I lost my child who I gave birth to with whom I had many dreams and plans for."

Someone else said : "Don't worry they are with God now..." I thought, " I love God, but I'm in pain right now and the idea that they are anywhere else kills me and what if I didn't believe in God, how would that help?"

Another said " It will take a few months for you to get over this" I thought " A few months are you crazy?! I will never get over this"

One said " I know how you feel" I thought " No you don't, you could not possibly know how I feel."

Another said " When my dad passed I felt the same way" ME: " No, I'm sorry it's not the same." Everyone grows up and has the idea that one day they will bury their parents, but no one plans to bury their child." I lost my Dad and I miss him, but in no way can I compare the losses. My dad was expected to get older one day and go before me, but not my Son.

Another said " Well at least you have other children" ME: " Yes I may have other children, but sometimes they remind me even more that I lost one. When I go to call them to say something about my day I hang up and then I sometimes go to call my Son to tell him too and then I realize that I can't call him anymore."

One said " I'm a mother too and I know just how you feel." ME: " No Sweetie, you didn't **LOSE** a child, so stick with ' you can't imagine.'"

Another said " He has no pain now.." ME: " Oh did someone come down from the heavens and tell you that? I am sure he has no pain, but during my loss, the only thing I could see was the pain, I kept hoping he didn't suffer."

Another said " They are in a *happier* place." ME: " Thank you, but my child was already in his happy place enjoying his life with his family. I am aware that God is good, but I still wanted my Son with me."

People do not understand that just a simple **" I'm sorry for your loss."** Is the best thing to say. Then keep quiet. It is an unfathomable loss and unless you have experienced this loss your words can cut into the parents and family like a knife.

Things to Remember

Losing a child devastates the entire family, (Mothers, Fathers, sisters, brothers, Aunts, Uncles, cousins, Grandparents). **Everyone grieves differently**. Some people need space and some people need to have a lot of attention and closeness. **Try** to keep your marriage and strong and try to not let the loss break that strength. **Don't worry** about what others say, they are not in your shoes, they know nothing. _Always try to honor the Child that you lost and in that, you keep them Alive._ All of our lost children matter and they will always exists in our hearts and minds. _Be kind to yourself_ because this is an **EXTREME** loss. If you have spirituality, hold on to it as it becomes very resourceful. **Forgive** those who do not understand, keep your distance, but forgive. Please do not blame each other, this is the time everyone needs more love. **Allow** each other to mourn however they need to and for as long as they want. **Talk** to your child whenever you can, they are still here, only now in spiritual form they hear us and see us all the time.

People Acted As If Losing A Child Was Contagious

Sometimes it felt as if people were afraid to hear about my Son, I think they might have been afraid of thinking that they could also lose a child. Seeing what happened to me must have been a constant reminder in which their greatest fear of losing a child could actually happen to them. I would mention my Son and they would quickly change the subject or they would just look at me with sympathy and pity. Some of them had to avoid me because they didn't know what to say. For the most part most people were supportive of what I was going through and they let me bring him up whenever I wanted and that felt great.

It is true that at any given moment it could happen to anyone, but for not it was just happening to me and my family. People have suggested to me that I should go out more and maybe meet someone, "Go out and meet someone?" and do What? I was in no position to meet anyone and start a relationship. I had to figure out who I was, never mind figuring out someone else. Then I was told to go right back to work because it would make me forget, "Forget?" Nothing will ever help me forget, you just don't forget you had a child. To tell you the truth I could care less about their opinions, they know nothing, and they didn't lose a child, I did what was best for me and in my own way.

Everyone in my family was grieving differently in their own way. My daughters never lost a Son and I never lost a sibling and my Son's Dad was never a Mother and I was not a Father. We may think we feel the same, but we really have had our own unique relationship with my Son Darien in a separate way. So, I try not to tell them how they should be grieving or what they should do.

Inside I was so broken and lost and yet on a higher level I truly believe that my Son has served his purpose and fulfilled what he was called to do in this lifetime. Even through his death there was a meaning underneath it all. When we lose someone we are brought to our bottom and on that bottom there is no way out but up. Sometimes from the worst of situations we grow and against the odds, we put ourselves back together again. And sometimes our pain and growth is for those around us to also learn and grow. All tragedies eventually lead to compassion. They bring out our concern and kindness and our deepest fear so that we can work on ourselves. Sometimes the people ahead of us prepare us for what is to come.

I can truly say that from the moment my Son passed, I no longer feared death, I almost welcome it now. Death to me now is another home that I just didn't get back to yet. I am here to grow spiritually by learning from others and developing my own compassion through pain and learning to understand that we all suffer differently. I found that some of the most beautiful people are the ones that have been through so much and yet still find a way to hold their head up and learn to walk on their new road of challenges. To be human we sometimes get lost with our ego and lose sight of what is really important. The more spiritual we become we slowly learn to let go and let God. Keeping the idea that God created everything we have keeps me grounded and helps me to remember that God always has the last say in everything.

Of course I would like things my way, but that is the human part of me and my ego gets in the way. Sometimes God sends us down another road so that we can somehow affect the lives of others so that we can eventually relate well with each other and develop an understanding and acceptance of one another.

My daughter Danelle called me today and she asked me if there are times when I feel weird when I think of Darien. She explained that it was a beautiful day and she thought of him and realized that he could not enjoy the beautiful day or be here with us ever again. I told her that I feel that way all the time and that sometimes I look at his picture or something of his and it brings everything up all over again. I told her that he cannot be here in physical form, but that he is always here in spirit and always around us. Sometimes I think of all the bad people out there and for a second I think, "Why my Son?" he didn't smoke, rarely had a drink, never did drugs and was so kind and helpful to others.

But I only go there for a second because my beliefs come back into focus and then I realize it has nothing to do with good or bad, sometimes when things happen to a bad person people learn nothing from it because they say things like "oh well, they were so rotten, or they did drugs." The truth is that we learn so much more when things happen to good people because then it hits home. We become afraid that we could lose our own good people at any time. Also death is part of life and no one is spared. We think we are losing something if we die, but it's the other way around, we actually gain more perfection for our soul to grow even more beautiful. God is not out to hurt us and yet we are all so afraid of facing our last day here. Imagine how God must feel.

My daughter Dakota Rose asked me "Who will be there when Darien arrives?" because he doesn't know anyone and he might not remember Grandpa Fred (my Dad). So I ventured again into the writings of reincarnation and it says that when someone dies they will see whoever they need to see in order to feel comfortable when they arrive, which explains even if their parents are alive another soul or souls will take on the images and the personalities, of their parents or friends so they feel safe to adjust and follow through on their journey in heaven and until they are comfortable and know where they are and remember their purpose for being on earth.

It made me feel calm to think that he might have seen both of his sisters, along with me and his Dad. It explains that sometimes a very passionate soul can have a hard time letting go of their time on earth and to avoid going into shock or crisis they may need to be greeted by their earthly family long enough to be able to adjust into the spiritual part of their soul. I know for sure that when my Son died, that at some point he was at first very upset and probably would have chosen to stay here longer. It is said that people with very strong personalities who are attached to earthly things and passions have a harder time letting go of their earthly life and that was my Son, he lived like he was never going to die.

The human part of me does not accept losing my Son, I want him back and I feel cheated and robbed of a future that I had planned much differently than the way it turned out. But the spiritual part of me understands that God has a reason and a plan and it is always in our best interest for the optimal spiritual growth of our soul.

Sometimes Doing Nothing is Alright

There were so many days that I could not participate in any situation or with anyone. I didn't want to go out anywhere. I only made it to my mailbox or to the grocery store. I felt that no one understood me and what I was going through. Most of my family and friends would say that I was such a strong person and I guess I was stuck with their expectation of me being so strong, but I was not so strong and I could not fall apart on those people who had this "she's okay" stamped on me. I was not okay in any sort of way, there were so many times I thought that if I were to stop breathing it would be okay. I was tired , very tired and broken and I mean really broken. There were so many times when I wished I was no longer here. But my belief in reincarnation keeps me from the crazy thoughts and will not let me leave on my terms, as I have a purpose for being here and only God decides when that purpose is completed.

Being alone was a bit of a torture, but it somehow had some sort of meditative value. It was easier to sit alone and think by myself without anyone else trying to give me their opinions on how I should get past this. For over a year I kept to myself, I woke up, took walks, ate and went back to sleep. Sometimes I even slept for most of the day, I was in a slump because before this I was very active and hyper. I was doing standup comedy and I could not bring myself to get back up on stage. My whole life was making people laugh and now I just didn't want to. I told myself that I would not do comedy for at least a year and in four months it will have gone into two years. Everything was funny to me until the most serious of things happened and at that point nothing seemed funny. I have continued to write and I will do comedy again, when I am ready.

I must say that from a very young age I questioned life, I noticed how individually different we all are. I went to Catholic School and Church and through my own perspective I found there to be a lot about the religion that didn't add up. I found some of the most religious people to be the most judgmental. I realized that we are who we are by location, parents, and outside influences. I am not part of any specific religion, I am a human being put here on earth to grow and develop into the best human being and grow spiritually. You see, I could not believe in a God that wasn't fair. I could not understand why there are very poor people who have nothing and very rich people who have everything. So I eventually became intrigued with different religions and their beliefs and the one that I found to make sense to me and be the fairest was Reincarnation along with Karma, because it made more sense as to why sometimes the worst things happen to the best of people.

In reincarnation it is said that we will eventually live each other's life and at some point or another we will face any and all of the trials and tribulations that others around us have gone through, but through different lifetimes. We are all here to live out as many lifetimes as it takes to become complete and pure like God and then we return when we are just as forgiving and loving as God is. That beforehand we agreed to the life we now live, hard as it may be and feel at times. That our families will relive many lifetimes with us and that our roles will change in each lifetime.

It says that some of the most difficult people we meet help us to grow the most and teach us to have compassion and to forgive. I believe that is why there are so many ups and downs and life is continuously changing so that we are not burnt out from one situation and can continue to grow. For me I find solace in that belief and it keeps me from being angry at God because it makes me realize that things are not happening to me only and that each and every one of us has a cross to bear. That all of us are broken, but not at the same time. Our neighbor can be living a very happy life while we are suffering on our own, and then two months later the tables change and we are living a happy life and our neighbor is now devastated and suffering. That is where we have the chance to be less judgmental and more compassionate. It seems so hard when we feel down for us to look out into the world and see people who seem so happy, we forget that their happiness doesn't last long, as something else comes along and there is a new lesson to be learned.

Everyone we meet was set up to be in our life long before we were even born, and we actually chose our parents to be our parents and no matter what they were like they helped make us who we are, Good or Bad. They were exactly who they were supposed to be so that we could learn from the experience. I didn't have the best situation growing up, but I like who I am. So I am thankful that my parents were exactly who they were in order for me to become who I am. The one thing I mostly learned from them were my morals and principles and that was a gift, I knew I was an old soul from a young age, as I was a very deep thinking child.

My girlfriend Ann Marie used to make fun of me and tell me that I was never a child and that I was more like an adult mother as a friend. That I was always trying to get others to do the right thing. It's so true because while most of my friends were drinking or getting high I was usually sitting next to them trying to talk them out of it, by telling them about the dangers of what could happen to them. I never understood why people felt the need to escape reality.

As I come to the ending of my story about the loss and experience of losing my Son, I realize there can never be a happy ending because the truth is my Son Darien is still physically gone and the pain that I feel from missing him is still there and will always be there. I am very thankful to have been fortunate enough to have an awareness that my Son is still near me and can see and hear me all the time and I believe that there is a little comfort now knowing one day he will be there when it is my turn to leave this earth. As a human being and Mother my heart still feels like it is going to rip open and the pain remains as I fall into pieces. Especially times when I watch the rest of the world go on and I see a Mother and Son in the parking lot and her Son is helping her with the groceries. I ask " Where is my Son?" Or I see guys his age at the beach and having fun while running through the sand I ask " Where is my Son?"

I'm truly happy for those who still have all their children, but the pain shows up whenever I see a family with a boy his age. It's such a bittersweet feeling where at first I am thankful for the memory and yet at the same time I can't face the reality of it, but I must go on and cherish the memories I do have because some day we are all going to be a memory. So my life exists now for my two beautiful daughters who I love more than words could ever say.

I have let so much of me focus on the death of my Son, and I now realize that I also have to focus on the (Life) of both my daughters. They are here, living and breathing right in front of me and I still have to be their Mom until I leave this world. They are going to have so many beautiful times and occasions happening in their future of which they will celebrate and I intend to be a big part of all those moments and to express a true happiness for their future lives.

13. MY SON'S FRIENDS

My Son's friends were so eager to help in any way they could and they were all so sweet in coming up with so many different ideas on how they could honor my Son. They had made car decal stickers, it was a picture of my Son on his motorcycle and they gave them out to our immediate family. I liked them so much I ordered more for a few other people. They were so awesome, every time I got into my car I would notice my Son's picture decal on the back window of my car and it made me feel as if he were with me whenever I drove my car. They also made us T-Shirts with his face on them which I keep mine over one of my pillows which helps remind me to keep up with my ritual of saying goodnight to my Son.

Many of his friends stop by his memorial site and add flowers or little tokens to express their love and loss of him. Some of them even clean up the area, as it is still beautiful looking almost two years later. Right after my Son passed they did a motorcycle run where so many of his biker friends road in and formed a circle while a drone flew over all of us and filmed the who memorial. It was so beautiful. There were more than 130 people. My Son probably had tears falling from his eyes while watching everyone show up. So much planning and effort and it was done in such a short time, they even had sky lanterns which they gave us and they sold the rest of them to other friends and we all sent one up into the sky for my Darien. I remember silently saying to my Son "Look at all these people who were so affected from losing you, you were very loved and you mattered."

For Darien's 1st Anniversary my family planned another memorial and I bought the sky lanterns and asked his friends to come, a year later and I think about eighty to a hundred people showed up, it again was so beautiful. He had friends that came from Queens and Manhattan and all over Long Island. It was so amazing to see all of the support. I gave each of his friends a silver charm necklace of a guy on a motorcycle and they all really liked it. For some of the closer friends I gave them a small glass vial with my Son's ashes in it. They were so thankful when they got the ashes, a few of them said they will feel as if my Son was watching over them while they ride.

I will never get to thank each and every one of them because there were so many, I am so thankful for the dedication, effort and time they put into helping our family have something positive and beautiful to remember Darien with. They helped me and my family focus more on my Son's life and all the beauty, then on his death and all the overwhelming sadness. I was so proud of my Son to have made such great friendships with such incredible and beautiful people. God bless them all and keep them safe.

Special thanks to "Sid Draper Mundo", The artwork that you made of my son Darien is so Sacred to me, it's the first thing I go to in the morning to say hello to Darien and at night I do the same thing when I say goodnight to him. It's by my front door and I cannot leave or enter my condo without seeing it. A while back a medium mentioned some type of artwork that someone made either in plastic or glass and that it was by one of our doors and that he enters through that, he also said that my Son thought the artwork was really special. Thank you so much, I will treasure it for the rest of my life.

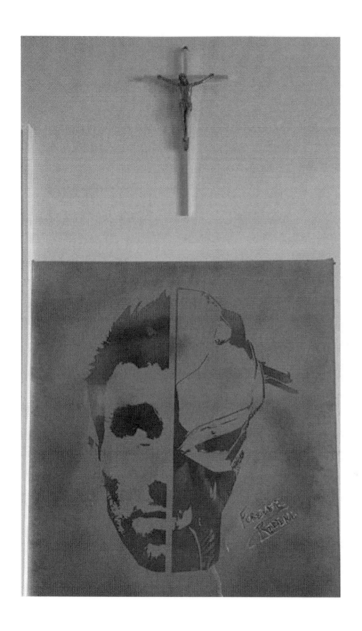

This Amazing Artwork was Done By Sid Draper Mundo.
Thank You Again Sid.

Darien and Friends doing what he loved

Darien loved all his Friends

14. IN HONOR OF REBECCA

On November 17th, 2016 while writing this book I received a phone call from my daughter Danelle, and she said, "Mom I have to tell you something and I don't know how to say it." So the first thing I said was, "Did anything happen to anyone in our immediate family?" all I could think of were my children, my Mom, my sister, my brother and their families. My daughter answered, "No, but it's very heartbreaking and sad." So I told her to just tell me already. It was then at that moment that she told me that my friend Margie's daughter Rebecca was killed in an accident, she was struck by a tow truck driver and run over. I have to say I immediately related to everything I felt with losing my Son. Everything came flooding back to me as if it were happening personally to me also, and it was.

The immense pain I felt took away my breath for a while and all I could think of was my friend and her family, as I already knew what they were about to face and go through. I had to stop myself from calling them right away even though it felt to me as if we were immediate family in that moment of knowing the pain they were in. My mind raced through the memories of when our families had met and got together. My Son and her daughter Rebecca knew each other and had lived on the same block and went to school together and at the age of 26 they both died in terrible accidents that took them quickly.

Rebecca was a sweet kid and she was very compassionate, caring and unique soul. Both of her parents were such good people, they were very supportive of her in everything that she did and always allowed her to be her own person. Her Mom had reminded me that when we first got to know each other that I had told her that her daughter Rebecca was the female version of my Son Darien. It now seems to be so true as they were both very set in their beliefs and ideas and had similar outlooks on being so open to anyone from any background and age. They were both very good friends to their friends and both of them were highly like by so many people and they had so many friends. To me I feel they were old souls and they knew so much more than most people their age and on a deeper level. To this day my heart aches for both my Son and Rebecca. She was not my child, but I remember feeling so proud of Rebecca for being strong enough to be different and not change who she was and what she believed in because of unhappy, judgmental people. In the end the truth always prevails and people respect you more for sticking to your own individual plan.

I feel so deeply connected to her Mom through all of this loss, we lived on the same block and our children played together. Who knew we would both have such a horrible loss. I truly believe that my Son welcomed Rebecca when she arrived and I believe they are together watching over us until we get there one day. When you lose a child you are in pain all over again when another parent loses their child, it's like an echo that comes back from the sound of your own original pain. God Bless my friend Margie and her family, it's going to be a long emotional road ahead.

15. LETTERS FROM HIS SISTERS

A LETTER FROM HIS SISTER DAKOTA ROSE

To my beautiful, daring, fun and loving brother Darien Grasman,

I'm not sure if I will ever be able to explain the immense amount of pain and absolute heartbreak this horrible reality brings me. I'm not sure I even believe this all yet. I know I already miss you like crazy. You are such a wonderful soul and I don't know how to take each coming day knowing that I can't call you quick or text you to see what you are up to.

Anytime we spoke, even if it were for only a few minutes, you would invite me to hang out with whoever you were already with, wherever you were, (whether it be hanging out doing nothing but watching TV, ordering food and talking , or you asking me to go to the Hookah Lounge at 3AM) (ha-ha). You were always so happy to introduce me to your friends and be out together.

I'm so sorry I didn't take more advantage of those times. It sickens me to think I'll never be able to see your smile or hear your hilarious (mostly kinda stupid ☺) jokes that crack me up beyond belief. You can put anyone in a better mood just by simply being you. We always said we were so alike and that always made me so happy. I have always been and will always be proud to call you my big brother.

I just hope that wherever you may be now, you aren't scared and instead you're happy and free. It's so hard and confusing because I wish you were with us to get through all this together right now and you just aren't. Life is so confusing and unfair sometimes. I love you so much Darien, Danelle Renae and I know how much you love us. You are with us forever. I'd like to thank everyone who reached out to support my family in this extremely tough time. We love you, we all know Darien made a new friend (Or Three ☺) everyday, so please feel free to come and see our lovely Darien one last time together.

Love,

Dakota Rose

A LETTER FROM HIS SISTER DANELLE RENAE

I am not exactly sure where to start. I do not even know where to begin with trying to describe the loss my family and friends have suffered. The thought of Darien not being in my life anymore tears my heart apart and leaves an empty feeling in my soul that I cannot describe. Darien was one of the most outgoing people I have ever known. He had a special ability to make friends with anyone and everyone, regardless of their age, gender or race. He brought new people into his life everyday with open arms and no judgment.

Darien was one of those people who excelled at anything he put his mind to. He always had a new hobby he was getting into. If he had an interest in it, he would go above and beyond to become the best at it. I was always impressed with how dedicated he was with anything he put his mind to. Darien was an all or nothing type of person when it came to learning about new things. He made sure that he knew everything there was to know about anything that he got into. He would do his research to make sure he had the best of the best, top- notch gear, parts, tools so he could be as close to perfect as he could be.

He was always a daredevil, always testing the limits. I will never forget the time we were being babysat and he tried to convince me to climb out of our bedroom window to sit on the roof with him. He tried to assure me that holding on to the blinds pull cord would keep us from falling. Of course he went out to sit on the roof and once my parent's got home I ran to rat him out. What else are younger sister's for?

I believe his love for extreme sports began with BMX biking. I remember him hanging out in front of the house every night working on his BMX bike and building bike ramps that were better and higher to do crazy tricks off of.

And then he got his driver's license. It was no surprise that the next love of his life was drifting. His first car was a 1990 Toyota Camry and he still did as much work to the car as he could to sup it up. I remember he was so excited to show me the new chrome shifter knob he installed in it.

I feel that no other hobby in Darien's life could come close to his love for motorcycles. I wouldn't even consider biking one of Darien's hobbies, it was his passion.

I wish I could honestly say that I am not mad at him for falling in love with biking. But I realize now that Darien lived his life to the fullest, seizing every moment of it and filling it with his passions. I cannot say that many people live their lives that way.

Darien was the most funny, caring, and lovable brother that I could ever ask for. Darien, Dakota and I could have fun together no matter where we were, just acting goofy and stupid and making each other crack up. I loved every second that we all get to spend together; it was always full of love and laughter. I remember one day my mom was driving Darien, Dakota and I home from the dentist. Darien called my name and said "Watch This". He had a rubber band in his hand and flung it towards the front of the car and hit the back of my Mom's head. I decided I needed to one up him and found a plastic bag on the floor of the car. I blew it up and popped it right behind my Mom's head. Sorry Mom.

We had a bond that could and can never be broken. Darien, Dakota and I know that at a very deep level we are a unit, a loud messy loving and long-lasting unit. And whenever the need arose we were able to call on that strength. I believe that we are still able to be a unit. I know Darien is somewhere looking down on the both of us, and he is going to watch out for us every single day to make sure we are strong and feel his love.

I am truly devastated that he was taken so suddenly and way too soon, but I also cannot put into words how fortunate I am to have been given a brother like him, no matter how short the period of time I was able to spend with him. He was so carefree and light hearted, and knew exactly how to make me laugh and put a smile on my face. How much I miss him already is unbearable. The little things are what I am going to miss the most, like his smile, his laugh, his hug, his silly faces, the way he always joked around. He always made sure he told me that he loved me, whether in person or just after a quick phone call.

I want to thank each and every one of you for your support and condolences through this hardship that my family and I are enduring. It warms our hearts to know the influence he has had on so many people's lives. I truly know that he was loved by an endless number of people.

Love,
    Danelle Renae

Lori Grasman

What Siblings Go Through

They shutdown and cannot talk about what has happened

They painfully watch their parents suffer while focusing on the loss of their child

They can shut out other family members and go into a depression

They realize they will never get to be an Aunt or Uncle to that siblings Children

They also realize that their sibling will never be there when they have children

They might not want to talk about the death or have it brought up around them

They realize that family gatherings will never be the same

Sometimes they feel as if they could have helped to prevent what happened

They are reminded all over again when someone mentions their brother or sister

They realize that their texts and calls will never again reach the sibling they lost

They may even want to forget and block the memories to avoid pain from the loss

They avoid family gatherings because it reminds them that their family is now broken into pieces

They watch their parents change into different people.

Darien , Danelle and Dakota Rose at Danelle & Adam's Engagement Party July 11, 2015. Two Weeks Later our lives were drastically changed

16. MY OWN POETRY FOR DARIEN

Acceptance Poem

My Beautiful Son, with such a Beautiful Soul

My heart still beats, though it's no longer whole

I'm so proud of you my beautiful Baby, my Pookie

Be sure to give a big hug to Emma, Shadow, and Mookie

So much pain, it's so hard to breathe

But there are some things that I do believe

I believe that God has a reason for everything he does

And taking you away wasn't meant to hurt all of us

I truly believe he has a beautiful plan

Of which many of us don't understand

And although it feels really odd

I must live, let go, let God

I promise to tell you I love you every day and dream of you at night

Even though in my human mind I scream, this just isn't right

God how I want to pinch your face, kiss your cheeks and hold you tight

But the spiritual part of me isn't selfish, so I'm telling you my baby

To walk towards the light

And although this still feels so wrong

I say thank you, thank you God, for letting me keep you this long

Surviving The Mourning

For My Son Darien

You may have left this world

But you left your gifts to others

And though it broke my heart

Together we gave a smile to other Mothers

Because of you my Son, Someone has the Gift of Sight

They will get to see all they have missed, every day and every night

And for every muscle that held your heart

You will have given someone a longer life, A brand new start

And for some burn victims out there who can't even look at themselves

no more

You will have given them the courage to look in the mirror with more

hope than before

For me I am left with a beautiful, yet heartbreaking memory, of your life

so shining bright

And a gratefulness to have such a beautiful Baby, Boy, Young Man

Who brought such a depth of meaning to my life

Love Always.............. Mom

Lori Grasman

The Love Remains

My hearts blood is rushing through my veins

As they hand me a box that is holding *your remains*

I remember your body, your weight, and your height

As I look at this small box, I think it feels so light

I decided to share *you* with family and friends

In honor of you and so that the memory of you never ends

I'll look for you in everything that I see

As *I'm sure you will* be smiling and looking over me

Both in different places, we will keep an eye on each other and pray

That there will come a time we will be together, again one day

For all that you are, you were and for all that you have become

I'll love you till *my dying day*, my precious, precious Son.

This song is the most Beautiful Song ever made for a parent that has lost a child, it will always remind me of how I feel about losing my Son, Darien.....

My Son I Love You: By Preston Hall

In My Dreams You are Alive and Well, Precious Child, Precious Child

In My Mind I See You Clear As A Bell, Precious Child, Precious Child

In My Soul There is a Hole That Can Never Be Filled, But In My Heart

There Is Hope, Cause You Are With Me Still

In My Heart You Live On, Always There, Never Gone

Precious Child You Left Too Soon

Though It May Be True That Were Apart

You Will Live Forever In My Heart

In My Plans I was The First To Leave, Precious Child, Precious Child

But In This World I Was Left Here To Grieve, Precious Child, My Precious Child

In My Soul, There Is A Hole That Can Never Be Filled, But In My Heart

There Is Hope And You Are With Me Still

In My Heart, You Live On, Always There, Never Gone, Precious Child You Left Too Soon

Thought It May Be True That We're Apart, You Will Live Forever In My Heart

God Knows I Want To Hold You, See You, Touch You, And Maybe There's A Heaven and Someday I Will Again

Lori Grasman

Please Know You're Not Forgotten Until Then, In My Heart You Live On,
Always There, Never Gone, Precious Child You Left Too Soon, And
Though It May Be True That We're Apart, You Will Live Forever In My
Heart

Me, My Son Darien and his sisters, Danelle and Dakota Rose

17. MY THOUGHTS WHILE ENDING THIS BOOK

I can only speak for myself and from my own experiences, going back to when I was very young I always believed that there was a higher power (God) and that whatever he did, there was a purpose involved. I never realized how far my faith would take me. To my own surprise I found myself trying to remain as humble as I could possibly be. I hope to see my Son again in a future lifetime and share more experiences with him. In this lifetime, his death taught me humility, I was so broken open over this that the humility and the realization that I could not change what happened made me able to survive the loss of him. I believe everyone in our life teaches us something along the way.

Anyone of us could leave here next and we have no choice but to accept that reality. I hope that I get to live out the rest of my life without something like this ever happening again. I couldn't imagine it. A friend of mine lost two children and my heart goes out to her, because she is suffering so much from it. As for me, I want to leave here long before my daughters do. That is the way it is suppose to happen in life. We as parents are supposed to be buried first.

I wholeheartedly believe that my Son is in a good place and that he is happy and that he wants me to grow from this and maybe help other people along the way. I had so many other plans for my life and losing my Son was never part of those plans. Through faith and love I have to trust that God's intentions are always about what is best for me and my family. And that someday we will get to see Darien again and tell him how much we love him.

As I come to the ending of my story about the loss and experience of losing my Son, I realize there can never be a happy ending because the truth is my Son Darien is still physically gone and the pain that I feel from missing him is still there and will always be there. I am very thankful to have been fortunate enough to have an awareness that my Son is still near me and can see and hear me all the time. I believe that there is a little comfort now knowing one day he will be there when it is my turn to leave this earth. As a human being and Mother my heart still feels like it is going to rip open and the pain remains as I fall into pieces.

DARIEN LIVED
AND
HIS LIFE MATTERED

HE LEARNED TO FIND EXCITEMENT
IN EVERY MOMENT OF HIS LIFE

Thank you for reading my book on Child Loss and the loss of my Child, I can only hope for this to be helpful to other parents and families who lost a child and may now realize they are not alone on this heartbreaking new journey. God Bless You and your family, always remember, no one gets to tell you how to grieve or for how long. We may grieve this loss for the rest of our lives and only those who have been in this situation can only truly understand what happens to our emotions and how our lives have been altered so drastically. On that night, whoever I used to be died with my Son and I was left to create a new me as I go along. I'm taking things one day at a time. I have no choice.

For Any Comments Email :

surivingthemourning@gmail.com

We were blessed to have Darien in our life, no one can control the unexpected. God Bless You and Your Family.

Made in the USA
Columbia, SC
25 January 2019